Give and Take

Give and Take

by Tricia Springstubb

An Atlantic Monthly Press Book
Little, Brown and Company
BOSTON   TORONTO

FIRST EDITION

Library of Congress Cataloging in Publication Data

Springstubb, Tricia.
  Give and take.

  "An Atlantic Monthly Press book."
  SUMMARY: Sixteen-year-old friends develop relation-
ships with various members of the opposite sex and
with each other as they grow towards maturity.
  [1. Friendship — Fiction] I. Title.
PZ7.S76847Gr   [Fic]   80-28463
ISBN 0-316-80785-0

ATLANTIC–LITTLE, BROWN BOOKS
ARE PUBLISHED BY
LITTLE, BROWN AND COMPANY
IN ASSOCIATION WITH
THE ATLANTIC MONTHLY PRESS

BP

Published simultaneously in Canada
by Little, Brown & Company (Canada) Limited

PRINTED IN THE UNITED STATES OF AMERICA

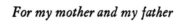

For my mother and my father

Chapter One

Dear Nome,

Do you believe this day? March 18th and it feels like May. We absolutely have to cut that assembly this afternoon and get outside — I'm ready to burst! Oh no, I think I see a robin — is that possible? What are you doing? I know, shorthand. "Dear Mr. Bla Bla: Regarding your order of June 19 . . ." I should be doing my chem but too bad. *My* science is watching that bird — I really do think it's a robin, Nome. I hope I'm a bird in my next life.

Write quick!

Love,
P.

First period

Dear Polly,

Yes, I was doing shorthand. *Trying* to, is more like it. That class makes me so nervous. Mrs. Leech goes so fast. Or could it be I go so slow? The words spin out of her mouth and POOF. They vanish into thin air before I can catch them. Somehow this seems the story of my life. My mother says, "No matter what, there will always be a need for good secretaries." She's probably right. Anyway I can't imagine what other kind of job I'd ever get.

About cutting assembly — I sort of would rather not, Pol. I was kind of looking forward to staring across the gym at

You Know Who for 45 minutes. I can hear you now — "You let Danny run your life!" Don't think I don't appreciate your advice — I mean what you said last weekend, when he and I auditioned for Big Time Wrestling in the back seat of his brother's car — what you said is true. About it being my body and my decision and all. But oh God, he's got that blue shirt on today, and it drives me crazy, he looks so good (to me, anyway). My mother says he's cute. I think she gets a real varicose thrill out of me having a boyfriend.

So please don't be mad if I don't cut.

Love,
Naomi

English

Dear Nome,

You mean vicarious.

Today's Words of Wisdom:

Shorthand: If it makes you so nervous and you hate it, why don't you just quit? Hand in your next homework, "Dear Mr. Bla Bla: Regarding your order of June 19, please take it and shove it . . ."

You and Danny: Aren't you going to watch him at lacrosse practice today? *Plus* you have to stare at him in assembly? I said it before and I'll say it again, You'll O.D. on him if you don't watch out.

Between classes just now Boom Boom gave me a St. Patrick's Day card. Only a day late. "Did you get it half price?" I asked. It's incredibly sentimental, all shamrocks and lace and rhymes about laughing eyes — I'm not sure what to make of the thing. He also ASKED ME SOMETHING VERY IMPORTANT AND I WON'T TELL YOU WHAT UNLESS YOU CUT WITH ME.

This day is doing weird things to me. Something keeps

tugging at me, like a dream I can't remember. Don't you hate that? Dreams are such strange things. It's so eerie, knowing there's a whole part of ourselves we can't control or understand. I'm not sure I like the feeling . . .

You're cutting assembly and that's that. I can't be left alone in this depraved condition.

me

Shorthand

Dear Pol,

Mrs. Leech is absent.

this space for silent thanksgiving

The sub is that young one, the one you say looks like DJ Lawrence. He opened a window and pizza fumes are blowing in from the cafeteria. My fat cells are jumping up and down saying, "Oh goodie goodie!" I guess I'll go to the library since I promised Danny I'd go on a diet and you know I can't resist *any* kind of pizza, even the tomato soup and cardboard kind they sell here.

What did Boom Boom ask you? Come on!

I don't ~~want~~ ~~think~~ ~~feel~~ know about cutting assembly. What if we get caught? And my mother finds out and I get grounded and I can't go out with Danny . . .

I never had anybody I liked like me back. Some days I'm afraid I'll wake up. Danny acts like a jerk sometimes, but underneath he's just like a little boy. He really is. I know you don't understand, Pol, but then we can't all be as popular

and beautiful as you are.

joke

ha ha

xxx,
Naomi

Dear Crazy,

D. *H*. Lawrence.

You know that assembly will be awful. The Italian exchange student will get up and give her little talk, then it'll be question and answer time and people will ask brilliant things like, "Is the pizza good over there?" Bor-r-r-ing.

Speaking of pizza, skip lunch if you want, but I'd never go on a diet just because someone told me I should.

Have you ever once got caught when you were with me? N-O. Get a pass to the girls room, and I'll meet you in the back parking lot. We'll fly.   ⟍   ⟋
　　　　　　　　　　　　　　　you　　　me

We can start our tans!

P.

Polly —

I never get tan. Only burned. But OK.

Chapter Two

They ran across the parking lot behind the school, through a little patch of woods, and darted out across the highway, Polly's red hair streaming out, flamelike, behind her. Naomi's saying she was worried about getting caught had just been an excuse. Polly never got caught, and when they were together her immunity rubbed off on Naomi like fairy dust, or the scales of a butterfly's wing. The great eye of misfortune winked when Polly went by.

They ran behind the bagel place, ducked through a hole in the fence, crossed a small patch of dead grass littered with broken bottles, and they were on the edge of Laughing Brooks, Polly's neighborhood. Acres and acres of identical ranch houses had sprouted on what used to be a farm. Naomi lived close by, but her neighborhood was much older, the houses all different from one another. "Your neighborhood is BVD," Polly liked to say. "Before Vapid Developments."

Laughing Brooks possessed no brook. The only water ran in the sewers beneath the streets, where younger kids still went to smoke. Little wreaths of smoke would rise up through the gratings into the street, like signals from some underground tribe. Once, when they were both eleven, Polly had talked Naomi into going down there with her. A few feet into the tunnel (you had to go to the sump to get in) Naomi panicked. She began to cry, and Polly had to lead her out. Naomi cried and cried, embarrassed and angry both at herself and at Polly, because of course Polly hadn't been afraid at all. Polly had put her arms around her and smoothed her hair, and never once did she tell anyone, or tease Naomi about it.

Bittersweet. If there was one word to describe Naomi's friendship with Polly, that would have to be it. They had known each other for seven years, ever since they were nine. One winter morning a new girl had appeared in Naomi's fourth-grade class, a girl who was all arms and legs and long red pigtails. Naomi was reading *Pippi Longstocking* then, a story about a girl who lived all by herself, no parents, just a pet monkey, and who ate candy all day and did whatever she pleased. This new girl looked just like Pippi. The fourth grade was studying the Vikings, and the new girl raised her hand first thing and announced she was an Irish-American and had red hair because the Vikings invaded Ireland in 795 A.D. Her mother said. "Well!" exclaimed the flustered teacher. "Well, well!"

At lunch that day Polly's tray was heaped with popcorn balls, tangerines, cupcakes, and cookies — offerings from kids anxious to make friends with the Viking. Naomi gave her a slice of her mother's choco-nougat cake, Naomi's favorite in all the world (still, though she now knew one slice had four hundred and sixty calories, and suffered guilt seizures every time she ate it). The icing had come off on the plastic wrap and Naomi watched Polly first scoop that off with one finger and lick it, then slowly, deliberately, eat the entire slice of cake. She licked her fingers again, thoughtfully. Naomi held her breath. Then Polly gave a slow smile.

"That," she said, "was the best of all."

"Really?" Naomi was beside herself with delight and pride — until she realized she'd just given away her favorite dessert.

Bittersweet.

It had been like that for seven years. Seven — was that supposed to be a lucky or unlucky number? wondered Naomi as they turned down Polly's street.

"And they're all made out of ticky tacky, and they all look just the same," sang Polly, striding ahead. Polly was slender and tall, nearly half a foot taller than Naomi, who had to take a few hopping, birdlike steps every yard or so, to keep up. "If one person in this neighborhood bought a life-size pink plaster elephant and put it on his lawn, within a week everyone else would have one, too."

"I don't know why you always have to make fun of your neighborhood," grumbled Naomi. Danny, in his blue shirt, would be looking for her across the gym. Wouldn't he?

"Why do you always have to be so critical of everything, Polly?"

"Who, me? I couldn't be critical of Jack the Ripper, not on a day like this. Look! Wasn't that a robin?"

"That? That was just a starling."

"Are you sure?" Polly skipped a few steps ahead, spun around once. She was wearing a dark printed blouse with pearl buttons, a very full black skirt that reached below her knees, and a quilted cotton jacket. Thrift-shop finds. Her thick, red-gold hair, held back from her face by two tortoise-shell combs, hung almost to her waist. Polly dressed in clothes she made herself or in things she rummaged out of church basements and tag sales: long batik skirts, silky blouses with lace collars, beaded sweaters, shirts embroidered with dragons and swans and tiger lilies. It was hard to say whether Polly was pretty or not. Her nose was long and had a bump in the middle; her eyes, though they sometimes flashed blue sparks, could just as often look plain dull gray. In photographs she sometimes looked quite homely. But when you knew her, when you'd been with her ten minutes, words like "pretty" didn't mean a thing. Polly had a way of altering the air around her, of diffusing the molecules and reassembling them just the way she wanted. Your perceptions went haywire when you were with her. She would take you outside at night and point out constellations: "See the bear, the swan, the queen in her chair?" You would say, "Oh yes, yes — look at that! Why didn't I notice them before?" The next night you would go out by yourself, and all you would see was what you'd always seen — handfuls of light, randomly tossed up in the sky. Had Polly made the hunter and the bear appear? Or were they still up there, but you were too dull to see them?

"I think it was a robin, Nome."

"I wonder if Danny's sitting next to Marcia Melon."

"He's staring across the gym, asking himself, 'Where is she? Did she go off with another guy?'"

"Ha ha."

"'Is she sick? Where is she?' He begins to panic."

"I wish."

"'What if something happened to her? I'll never forgive myself! To think of the way I treated her, in the back seat of my stupid brother's car . . .'"

"Stupid is right. That Donny drives me crazy. I think he's a bad influence on Danny. Every female that drives into his gas station has to be rated. 'Did you see that one?' he'll ask Danny. 'A Cadillac face on a Chevy body.'"

"Donny has the IQ of an after-dinner mint."

"I hate doubling with him and his girlfriend. *She* has the IQ of a doorknob. Their favorite thing is going to gruesome movies. She screams and hides her head on his shoulder, and he protects her by putting his hand down her shirt. That movie we saw last weekend, that showed the guy in the electric chair — that was the worst. Afterwards I tried to say I thought capital punishment was stupid, and two wrongs don't make a right, and Donny started going on and on: what did I know about hardened criminals, a naive girl like me. . . . I couldn't get a word in. And Danny goes right along with him. He acts so macho around Donny, not like himself at all."

"Well, why don't you stop going out with them?"

"I'm going to tell Danny I don't want to anymore. This weekend *I'm* taking *him* someplace."

"Where?"

"It's a secret. That reminds me — what did Boom Boom ask you today?"

"He asked me to the prom."

"Really? Already? It's months away."

Polly shrugged. "He has it on his mind. You know he'll probably be elected king. What do they call it in horse racing — the Triple Crown? He's already been elected class president and Mr. Sully, *the* male senior at Charles E. Sully High School. This'll be his final coup."

Naomi kicked a pebble ahead of her. "I wonder if Danny'll ask me. Juniors can go, too, you know."

"Proms," pronounced Polly, "are anachronisms. Like garter belts, and not kissing on the first date."

"Is that what you told Boom Boom?"

Polly nodded. "Only I added, 'I'll see.'"

"Maybe he won't wait for you to see."

"That's what he said, and I said, 'To each his own.' But I'm pretty sure he'll ask me again. Boom can't stand to take no for an answer. Besides, he can afford to wait. He could ask any girl in the school the day before the prom and she'd say yes."

"Allow me to touch the hand that touched the hand."

"Get out!" Polly ran up the front walk of her house. "Oh, let me out of these hot clothes!" She unlocked the front door and went in.

Naomi followed more slowly. It was convenient, having a mother who was a junior-high-school teacher and didn't get home till an hour and a half after you did. Polly's mother, Catherine Quinn, taught seventh-grade English. Naomi remembered having her, and being terrified the whole year. Her younger brother Gerald had Mrs. Quinn now. QUINN THE FIN he wrote on the paper cover of his English book, beneath a drawing of a shark. Mrs. Quinn was very strict. She said clear thinking depended on clear understanding of language. Naomi could still remember when they learned to diagram sentences. Day after day Mrs. Quinn covered the blackboard with what looked, to Naomi, like formulas for nuclear war. Naomi had spent the year scrunched down behind the boy in front of her, mumbling spells, trying to render herself invisible.

From down the hall, in Polly's room, came the scraping of a chair, the thudding of something heavy, and singing. " 'Dress yourself in sunshine . . .' "

Naomi made faces at herself in the hall mirror. If you only saw my head, you wouldn't know I was fat. She sucked in her cheeks. Danny says he likes the way I look. Love is blind. Love! Let's not be presumptuous, Ms. Denning. When does "like" turn to "love"? Or "girl" to "woman"? Does a bell go off and a flare shoot up? Naomi puffed out her cheeks. Now *that's* fat. Like Boom Boom used to be in fourth grade. He's come a long way, baby. Mr. Sully, a full-page photo of him in the Charles E. Sully High School yearbook. And he asked Polly to the prom. " ' 'Cause today is yours and mi-ine!' " Polly has such a pretty voice. Polly tells me, "Don't laugh when Danny says he likes the way you look. Why do you always laugh when people give you compliments?" Always, as if I'm getting compliments every other minute. A good question, though, as usual, from Polly.

Reflected in the mirror, behind her head, Naomi could see the Quinns' impeccably neat living room, the throw pillows on the couch standing up shoulder to shoulder, as if at attention. Mrs. Quinn was so proud of her house. She had earned it and everything in it herself. You wouldn't catch Polly making fun of the neighborhood when her mother was around. The only thing out of place was the skateboard sticking out from under the couch. That belonged to Cass, Polly's little sister.

Naomi began an exercise she had seen in a magazine. It was for double chins. "Stewed prunes," she said softly, jutting her chin at the ceiling and making a fish mouth, "stooooood prooooons."

"There, that feels better. Are you all right?"

Naomi turned, chin pointed in the air. Polly was wearing cutoffs and a T-shirt with a picture of a *Tyrannosaurus rex* on it.

"Stooooood prooooons," said Naomi. "It's my new isometrics."

"What if your face gets stuck that way?"

"You can do these exercises at your desk. I can reduce my thighs while I listen to Mrs. Rugchild blab about Metternich."

"I don't know how many times I've told you you're not fat. You are simply Rubenesque. Come on outside."

Polly got a can of soda from the refrigerator and they sat on the back steps. The yard was small but as neat and trim as the house. On the clothesline hung three pairs of jeans. The long skinny ones were Polly's, the double-knit ones her mother's, and the short chubby ones with the patch on each knee belonged to Cass. A starling, its wings iridescent purple and green, landed on the line, making the jeans sway slightly. *Veee-veeer,* it said.

"See, that's a starling," said Naomi. "They sound like squeaky hinges."

"What?" Polly sat with her head tilted back, her eyes closed, her hair making a red-gold pool on the steps where she rested her elbows. She stretched her bare legs, luxurious as a cat in a sunny window.

"Never mind." Naomi rolled her jeans up as far as they

could go. Dark hairs lay curved like parentheses up and down her winter-pale legs.

"Isn't this lovely? Isn't this better than sitting in that smelly gym?"

It was. The sun warmed the top of Naomi's head; the starling's wings glinted, neon green and violet. *Veee-veeer!* Its dull, colorless bill would turn bright yellow in a month or two, Naomi knew. In a month or two everything would change. The promise was in the air; you took a breath, and the promise was in you. Naomi picked up a fallen twig and traced Danny's initials in the dirt at the bottom of the steps. DN, the reverse of hers. DN + ND. Tomorrow she'd share her secret with him.

"You were right again, Pol Parrot. Why oh why do I ever doubt your wisdom?"

But Polly wouldn't be teased. POOF — like Mrs. Leech's dictation — she had escaped Naomi, slipped off into her own world. She had a knack for doing that. Now she sat with her eyes shut, a frown like a bird in flight lightly etched across her forehead. Naomi opened the soda, took a long drink, and held it out to Polly. But Polly didn't move.

"Do you think you might go to the prom with Boom Boom after all?"

No reply.

"I hope you don't catch pneumonia sitting out here like that. My mother says this is pneumonia season."

One bare foot gently rubbed the other.

"This sure is better than assembly. I sure do love drinking soda and talking to myself."

"Nome." The single syllable hung in the air like a gunshot. Even the starling froze.

"Huh?"

"I think I've figured out why I've felt so strange all day. As if I'm on the verge of remembering a dream, but can't quite."

Naomi gulped soda. "Yeah?"

"It was a day like this my father left us."

Polly didn't open her eyes. Naomi took another drink. "It was?"

"I never did tell you about the day he left us, did I?"

Chapter Three

"No," said Naomi, "you never did."

"The day my father left us," Polly said, "he threw all his clothes in our one and only suitcase — we were poor then, my mother likes to point out — put his telescope — he loved the stars, I remember that — in a shopping bag, walked right out the front door, past me shinnying up a tree and Cass playing in the mud, right past us without one word, around the corner and out of sight."

"And you never saw him again?"

Polly shook her head slowly. "For a while he sent us birthday presents and cards and that first Christmas a life-size stuffed goat, with wheels. Cass was terrified of it and my mother gave it away to the children's home. Every card said 'Love, Daddy.' I turned them over and over and inside out, but that was all they ever said. Then the presents slowly dwindled away and finally stopped and my mother said, 'Good riddance.'"

"Your mother is a strong woman."

"I know."

It was what everyone said about Catherine Quinn. It was as automatic a combination as "Hi, how are you? — Fine, and you?" Or, "World without end — Amen." When you mentioned Catherine Quinn, the reply was, "A strong and independent woman!"

The starling eavesdropped quietly, its gaudy wings folded. Naomi tried to imagine a fourth pair, a man's pair, of jeans on the line. Of course there had been a man once. Funny that you never thought of him, or tried to imagine what he was like. You almost imagined Polly and Cass had sprung into the world by spontaneous generation. A pair of men's jeans would look very odd on that line.

As if she could read Naomi's mind, Polly said, "He was wearing white pants." Her voice now was flat and colorless, a hypnotized voice, and Naomi began to feel nervous, the way she did when someone who was stoned told her secrets. People always regretted that, the next day. Polly never spoke about her father.   Noami doodled in the dirt.

"I can still see him so clearly! The pants were white, but the left leg was turned all gray. Later my mother told me that was because he stepped in the cat's dish on the way out. She said, 'You know he always wanted a dog instead of a cat. He turned that dish over on purpose.' I said, 'Don't be silly,' and she slapped my face. Oh!" Polly's eyes flew open, remembering that. At the sound of her "Oh!" the starling spread its wings and flew away. "I haven't thought of that in years."

"You haven't?" Noami hated how stupid her own voice sounded.

"No. It's strange, the way I think of him. When I think of him, if I think of him. I feel as if I'm watching a movie —

I feel as if it's happening out there someplace," Polly waved her hand, "to someone else."

"That's how I felt that time Stewart got hit by a car. I saw the whole thing happen, but I didn't believe it. I was waiting for the commercial to come on, or for someone to shake me awake."

Polly nodded. "Some things I remember about my father, I'm not even sure anymore if they really happened, or if I made them up. Like I think I remember him coming into the kitchen one night with his arms full of roses, and my mother yelling at him, 'Can we eat roses?' " She paused, shook her head. "But I'm not sure. She hardly ever talks about him."

Naomi finished the soda, and gave a tremendous belch. "Sorry," she whispered, embarrassed as if she'd farted during the sad part in a movie, or stumbled on someone crying. "Sorry."

Polly laughed. She gave herself a little shake, and emerged from whatever trance she'd been in. She tossed back her hair, rubbed the bump on her nose, and when she spoke her voice was back to normal.

"It's okay, Nome. It doesn't bother me, talking about my father."

"But you never do."

Polly shrugged. "No one in my house does, much. Cass hardly remembers him — she was only two, and my mother — Catherine always tell us, 'I'll answer any questions you have about him. As much as I can, that is, considering it's all ancient history now. I'll tell you one thing,' Catherine says. 'He was long on romance, short on finance.' " Polly tilted back her head, closed her eyes. "He loved to sing and hated to work. Once he had a job planting trees. That was his favorite, according to Catherine. He stayed at it six whole months. Do I remember him coming home with muddy knees . . . ?" Polly pursed her lips, then shook her head once more. "They met at a Knights of Columbus dance and were married six weeks later. Hard to believe, isn't it, knowing my mother? Now whenever she talks about him she bites all the lipstick off her lower lip."

Naomi had seen Mrs. Quinn do that. Little pink flecks stuck to her two front teeth, which were yellow — malnutrition as a child. "I can see where he wouldn't exactly be her favorite subject."

Just then there was a rumble of low thunder, a *sssssh* of air brakes: the elementary-school bus. Cass was home. Naomi jumped up. "I didn't know it was so late!" She rolled down her jeans. "Danny'll be looking for me." But how could she just up and leave Polly, after a conversation like this? "Come to lacrosse practice with me."

"Bor-r-r-ing." Polly opened her eyes. "And you know you think so, too."

"I know, but Danny asked me to."

"So," Polly grinned, "you don't do everything Danny asks you to, do you?"

Naomi blushed — she was as prone to blushing as other people are to hives or hiccups — and felt confused. Polly had switched moods just like that. Just when I'm thinking she needs to be comforted, Naomi thought, she starts joking around.

"Don't worry about me and Danny. Next time he gives me any trouble I'll just sit on him till he screams for mercy. Are you sure you don't want to come?"

Polly closed her eyes again and stretched her legs. "I told you I'm starting my tan." Freckles had already come out on her nose and cheeks — nutmeg dappling cream.

"I'm going out with him tomorrow, too. I'll call you when I get back. For an Instant Replay."

"Okay. Ciao."

"Bye."

On the side lawn Cass and a friend were running Spiderman tattoos under the faucet and sticking them on each other's faces. Cass, dark and round, with a grimy Band-Aid on each knee, had thrown her schoolbooks and heavy jacket down on the ground. When she spotted Naomi she raised her arms Dracula-like and rushed toward her. The spiderweb tattooed under her eye made Naomi jump, and Cass doubled over, laughing till she fell to the ground.

Chapter Four

There were two kinds of happiness, Naomi had long ago decided. One was the peaceful kind. It would suddenly come over her, for no reason she could understand, while she sat in homeroom on a winter morning, the walls whiter than ever with reflected snow, the heat hissing, watching John Whelan frown over his trig. Or it could steal upon her as she watched her little brother Stewart button up his sweater, concentrating, or when, as now, she was walking through Polly's neighborhood, where all the houses were so tidy, each with its house number displayed in curly wrought-iron script, its shrubs tucked safely under burlap for the winter, and a shiny car waiting, like a patient pet, in its driveway.

This peaceful kind of happiness was very different from

the other kind, the kind she felt when she turned the corner of the hall and saw Danny waiting for her. That was the wild, heart-beating, blood-blooming kind. This quiet kind had to do with everydayness, with things being as they should be, and with little details that suddenly stood out, lovely and precious in their ordinariness.

But today, though she was walking through Polly's neighborhood, and though she was on her way to Danny, Naomi felt neither kind of happiness. Today something nagged at her, as if she'd told a lie and gotten away with it.

I let Polly down. I let my best friend down.

But how? By not staying to talk about her father? Polly herself had changed the subject. She wasn't one to give away her secrets. "Icicle," Boom Boom Bottzemeyer liked to tease Polly. "You are long and cool and slippery as an icicle. No one can get hold of you." Other people called her that, too, behind her back — mostly guys who couldn't get her to go out with them, or girls who were jealous of her.

"Why do you hang around with Polly so much?" Danny had asked once. "You act like she hung the moon in the sky — how come? She's not anything like us."

The other kind of happiness, the blood-rushing-to-the-head kind, took hold of Naomi when he said "us." But then of course she defended Polly.

"She's not like anyone. Who else do you know who's writing a novel? Who was once approached on a street in New York City by a movie director, and he wasn't just a pervert, either, he showed her his card? Who else do you know who can make cream puffs and avocado face masques and has read all of *War and Peace,* not to mention every Christmas gets a present from Egypt where the guy she went out with in ninth grade lives now? Besides," said Naomi, "Polly and

I've known each other forever, since we were nine years old. She used to give me the creamy half of her Oreos."

If it wasn't for Polly I'd never have done half the things, or gone half the places, or met half the people I have. I'd still be wearing my hair in bangs, if it wasn't for Polly.

And I let her down.

How did you let someone like Polly down? Smart, funny, invited-to-the-prom-by-no-less-than-Boom-Boom-Bottzemeyer Polly?

Is it true what they say, we're all the same underneath?

Naomi came to the edge of Laughing Brooks, where the quiet streets intersected the highway, and waited for the light to change. She could see the small patch of woods and the high school beyond. Despite her uneasy conscience her heart began to pound. He'd be looking for her. She pinched her cheeks and bit her lips and ran a hand through her limp brown hair.

A long, lemon-colored car, chrome glinting in the sunlight, turned off the main road, and the driver, a thin, angular woman with red hair straggling across her forehead, waved to Naomi. Mrs. Quinn. Naomi waved back, automatically pulling in her stomach and standing up straighter. The one time she had tried to really talk to Mrs. Quinn, leaning across the kitchen table and beginning, "Just between you and I," Mrs. Quinn had interrupted with, "You and *me,* object of the preposition *between.* Yes, go on."

The light changed and Naomi ran across the road. *I abandoned Polly for Danny.* Through the woods, across the parking lot — there he is.

At the same moment she spotted him, Danny turned. He was just her height and shape, solid and square. Once someone had taken her for his sister, and ever since he'd called her "little sister."

He saluted her with his lacrosse stick. Naomi waved — and forgot everything else.

Polly sat, face tilted to the sky, sun pricking her eyelids with arrows of white and gold. Remember when you were small, how you closed your eyes and dug your knuckles into them, to make the colors bloom. Remember how you dug your fingers into your ears, so you wouldn't hear her crying, alone in the big double bed . . .

She slapped my face. She never did anything like that before, or since. Later she apologized. She came into my room and held me and rocked me. She had never done that before, either, or if she did I don't remember. He was the one who did that — that time I climbed up on the roof he spanked me good, then came into my room asking, "Did I hurt you? Did I hurt you, carrottop? Huh, Pumpkin?"

Like a small, warm bird, a breeze brushed her cheek. It was a blue day like this, a false spring day, when he left us. Without looking back. It would be nice to think he was afraid he'd change his mind.

She cried. She cried and then she raged, so violently Cass and I were afraid to cry ourselves. We could only watch her. She gave all his things to the Salvation Army. She cursed him for taking the telescope, the one thing she might have sold. She cursed herself for a fool.

And then it stopped, like a spent storm. Then came the babysitters, and going out to jobs she mocked, and school at night. A student teacher at thirty-one. Quinn the Fin, all the tears dried up.

Polly opened her eyes. Cass and her friend stood before

her, barely able to contain themselves, waiting for her to scream at the sight of their creepy tattooed bodies. But Polly calmly closed her eyes again, and they slunk off in search of other victims.

A blue day like this, that's why I think of it. Well, there's no use thinking of it any more.

Polly let her mind float, one image after another rising to the surface, the way they did before she drifted off to sleep. She saw Naomi, and a willow tree, and then that great ridiculous stuffed goat her father had sent them . . .

"Polly, come help me!"

It was her mother, coming up the walk with her arms full of groceries. Her red hair straggled across her forehead and cheeks, and Polly knew right away she'd had a hard day. She ran to help.

Chapter Five

"Are you hungry?"

"You know I'm always hungry."

"Like me. I eat anything that doesn't crawl off the plate."

"Not fried turtle. Not boiled sheep eyes."

"Maybe with enough ketchup."

"Not tailbone soup."

"Speaking of bones, I have one to pick with you."

"I didn't do it, I didn't do it!"

"Yes, you did—and now you must pay!"

Danny was still wearing his lacrosse shirt, green with a gold 49. He'd knotted his sweatshirt around his neck, but now, as they walked down the long front driveway of Charles E. Sully, he untied the sweatshirt and twisted it between his hands. Naomi laughed nervously, and started walking backward.

"What, what did I do?"

"You know. You weren't in assembly. Where were you?"

"Wouldn't you like to know!"

Danny gave the sweatshirt another twist and flicked it out at her. Naomi screamed, ran a few steps ahead. "I was with Polly!" she laughed. "I went to Polly's house!"

"Why didn't you tell me? Huh? I was going to sneak across and sit with you!" He flicked the sweatshirt again, and Naomi screamed again, in pleasure-fear.

"I'm sorry, I'm sorry, I'll never do it again!"

"Promise?"

"Cross my heart!"

"Well, all right." He slung the sweatshirt back around his neck and grabbed her hand. "Donny promised to pay me today. We'll go to Steer Inn, okay?"

"Whatever you say, Forty-nine."

"Little sister."

They walked along streets Naomi had walked along too many times to count, but it was different, walking them with her hand in Danny's. When she was with him, every place they went seemed to become her own.

"Yow!"

He'd gotten her after all! He ran ahead, laughing, the sweatshirt streaming out behind him like a superhero's cape.

"That's just to make sure you learned your lesson!"

"I'll learn you a lesson!"

And the chase was on. Up one street and down another, until somehow Naomi was ahead, and it was Danny who was chasing her. She ran for her life, all the rest of the way to the gas station, her heart pounding so she wondered if sixteen-year-old girls could have heart attacks. At last she threw herself against the crumbly concrete wall of the station, panting, gasping, her hair in her face, laughter searing her throat. Danny stood over her, one arm on the air pump.

"You," she managed to gasp, as if it were a whole sentence.

"You," he said back, and his laugh was a low chuckle, like the sound the smooth sea stones make when the tide bumps them together. He bent to kiss her — and a greasy, grinning face materialized over his shoulder.

"So this is what I pay you for."

Donny. Danny's big brother, part owner of the station. Macho Man to the nth power. Danny kissed Naomi anyway, and she knew it was just for Donny's benefit.

"So this is what I pay you for, ha ha." A broken record.

"You *didn't* pay me yet."

"I've got one more oil change for you."

"Do you mind waiting?" Danny asked her.

"I like to watch you work."

"Sure she does. She likes to watch you earning the bucks to take her out. It's the blue Plymouth — use the ten-forty."

"This'll only take a minute," Danny told her.

"I don't mind."

He pushed up the sleeves of his lacrosse shirt and began draining the sluggish black oil. She did like to watch him work. Danny knew everything about cars. Someday he and Donny planned to have their own station, D & D's. When Danny was working on a car there was a calm, almost serene air about him, the air of someone who loved what he was doing, and knew he was good at it. That kind of competence fascinated Naomi, who could have trouble unfastening her seat belt.

Still, cars bored her (bor-r-r-ring, she could hear Polly drawl), and now that the sun was low she began to get cold. She hopped from one foot to the other, and considered telling Danny she really didn't appreciate being kissed just for his dim-witted brother's benefit. Polly would tell him.

"Almost done," said Danny, walking by with a new oil filter. She leaned against the car, watching as he put it on. How could he be so casual, messing around in there like that? She'd be afraid something would explode. More than once Danny had patiently explained the principle of internal combustion to her, and Naomi, pretending to understand, had nodded just the way she did when Miss Hoop explained how to score in tennis.

She watched him pour in the clean, amber-colored oil. On the back of his left hand was a scar he'd gotten years ago when he broke his mother's favorite lamp and tried to fix it before she found out. There are still so many ways he's like a child, she thought — the way he laughs, the way he gets so excited over something and insists I get excited, too, the way he tries to act bigger and tougher than he really is. Once as they were watching TV together Naomi had seen tears come into his eyes when some children's pet bird died. Danny didn't know she'd seen; she'd never tell him. Naomi smiled to herself. Polly didn't know that other side of him. She decided not to say anything about the kiss. In a few minutes they'd be away from here, and Danny'd be himself again. He scrubbed his hands, and they were bright red, like the hands of a child just out of the tub, when Donny counted his pay into them.

At Steer Inn Danny bought her a Bruiser Burger and a large Coke.

"I thought you wanted me to go on a diet!"

"You can start tomorrow." He bit into his first Bruiser, then suddenly laid it down and looked at her. "Tomorrow! Tomorrow's Saturday, I'm off, and we didn't decide what we're going to do!" Then he laughed. "Uh-oh, there she goes, the world-champion blusher. It's too bad they don't have an Olympic Blushing Event, you'd walk off with the gold." He picked up his burger. "How about going to see that new mad-scientist movie? It's supposed to be really bad." He pulled the neck of his shirt up over the back of his head, bared his teeth, and crossed his eyes.

"I was kind of thinking, since it's such nice weather . . ." Naomi rolled an empty straw paper across the table with one finger, feeling her blush get even deeper. "I was kind of thinking of taking you somewhere."

"Where?"

"A surprise."

He tore into his second burger. "But Donny said he'd drive us."

"Oh, you'll like this place, Danny, I know you will."

"It's not some place I have to wear a tie, is it?"

Naomi laughed. "You have to wear your oldest, raggediest clothes. And we have to go in the morning. That's when it's most beautiful."

"Okay, I guess I'll trust you, little sister." He drained his Coke, then reached over, grabbed a napkin, and scribbled on it. Like an Olympic judge he held it up, scrawled with a big red *10,* and presented it to her.

Chapter Six

He was late. Sitting on her front steps waiting, Naomi bit at the wart that had mysteriously begun to appear on her thumb. She spun the pedals of her bike around backward and did her thigh-reducing isometrics. Her mother came out and asked why this boy didn't have manners enough to come up and knock on the door instead of making her sit outside and wait, and Naomi said this was the twentieth century, for God's sake, and her mother said don't say for God's sake. For gosh sake then, said Naomi. For the hundredth time she jumped up and squinted down the street to the corner, trying to make him appear. Instead, Tess and Peter trudged into sight.

Tess and Peter rented three rooms in the upstairs of the Dennings' house. The most distinguishing thing about Tess and Peter, in Naomi's parents' view, was that they were Unmarried. JACOBI AND MALONE it said on their mailbox, penned in Tess's fancy Gothic script. Tess was an art student at the community college. Peter studied biology. When Naomi went up to visit them, Tess would usually be at her drawing table and Peter would be studying. He would read aloud some amazing fact from his text: A single cod lays nine million eggs a year, but fewer than half a dozen may survive. Tess and Peter were good tenants, quiet, for the most part, and they paid their rent on time. "Times change," Mr. Denning told his wife, but she shook her head. "Some things never change. Mark my words: he'll leave her. The girl is always the one to suffer."

At the moment, Peter looked like the one who was doing the suffering. Above his bushy red beard his face was drawn and tense, and as Tess went on talking his frown grew tauter and tauter, as if every word she spoke were another turn of the screw. Peter had fuzzy brown hair, so different in color and texture from his wiry orange beard that the beard almost looked pasted on, and he was tall and skinny. He ducked his head, listening to Tess. They both carried bags with leafy green vegetables spilling over the top. When they got close enough for her to hear, Naomi knew for sure that they were arguing.

"Hello, there!" she called loudly, to save them embarrassment when they noticed her.

Peter lifted his head, and she saw him try to focus, a swimmer surfacing from deep water.

"Naomi Macaroni!" His jolly tone was so artificial it made her wince. "What are you doing here all by yourself? Where's pretty Polly?"

"She works at Wally's Market on Saturdays. Been to your food co-op?"

Tess nodded. Her short dark hair was dusted with wheat germ. Naomi sometimes thought she'd look a little like Tess, if only she could lose ten pounds. This morning there were rings beneath Tess's big brown eyes.

"You're just the person I wanted to see," Peter went on, super-hearty. "You know how to grow an avocado, don't you?"

"Sure. It's easy."

"It is, huh? Then how come our apartment is full of glasses of stinking green water and slimy pits? I want to grow one for Tess, but I don't know if I can look another avocado in the face."

"You must be doing the pit upside down," said Naomi.

"Ha!" burst out Tess, the first sound she'd made. "That would be just like him."

Peter looked as stricken as if she'd hit him. This was bad.

Now it was Naomi's turn to pretend nothing was wrong. She gave her burgeoning wart a thorough examination. Peter drew a breath, about to reply, but just then Danny glided up, squeaking his brakes and just missing hitting Naomi's knee.

"Danny Peter Tess — Tess Peter Danny — are you ready let's go."

"Aha!" Peter gave her a huge wink. Really, he could be as corny as her father. "So this is why she's not with Polly today," he said, turning to grin at Tess. But Tess had disappeared.

"Who was that?" asked Danny as they pedaled away.

"A friend," she answered, and hoped he was jealous.

They rode out of her neighborhood, along the border of Laughing Brooks, up onto the highway, past the small cluster of stores where Mr. Denning had his dry-cleaning business. Half a mile past there they turned off the big road into a narrow lane with no street sign, where the houses were all set far apart. After another mile even the houses ended, and for a long space there was nothing, nothing but patches of strawberry and potato fields and clumps of woods, the trees studded with bright yellow NO TRESPASSING signs. Naomi's heart began to beat a little faster.

"Wait'll you see the skunk cabbage."

"The *what?*"

"You'll see."

Danny rode no-handed, arms dangling loose at his sides, humming the song that was number one, "Part-time Lover." His dark hair made little curls like lapping waves along the back of his neck.

"Mrs. Daniel Nicholson," Naomi whispered to herself, then tried, "Ms. Naomi Denning-Nicholson." The wind caught up her words and flung them back over her shoulder, and she laughed and began to sing along with him:

She says, "Sometimes I need you, love,
Other times I gotta leave you, love" —
But I don't want no part-time lover.

They left their bikes beside a paper birch, beneath a NO
TRESPASSING sign informing them they would be prosecuted
to the fullest extent of the law. *Ping!* Danny bounced a pebble off it.

"There's a little path."

It was warm, the ground just beginning to thaw, and there
were animal tracks in the thin top layer of mud. As they
walked along, holding hands, they left their own tracks,
their footprints almost exactly the same size.

"Those are rabbit tracks. And see this? It's called staghorn
sumac. Don't the branches look like antlers?"

"What'd you say? Why are you whispering?"

Danny's booming voice made her jump. "I didn't know I
was. I don't usually talk when I come here. I always come
alone."

"This'd be a great place to have a party. How'd you ever
find it?"

"It was a few years ago. I'd just had a huge argument with
my mother, and I jumped on my bike and rode and rode
till finally I looked up and found myself here. I wasn't here
five minutes before I forgot what I was mad about. This place
has a way of . . . of making me feel in love with the world."
She gave him a sideways look. He was breaking a dead
branch from a tree. "Did you ever see a wildflower, Danny?
A flower that grew in the middle of nowhere, for no reason?"

With a loud crack the branch came free, and he began
using it for a walking stick, gauging the mud with its tip.
"So this is your secret, huh?"

"I never brought anyone here before."

"Not even Polly?"

"Nope. Nobody but you."

He whacked a tree with his stick. "It sure is quiet here."

"I know. It's hard to believe we're just a few miles off the highway. Guess what we can find here. Trillium. It's a beautiful, beautiful flower, with three of everything."

"I didn't know you were a botanist," he said, and pulling her to him he kissed her, quick and hard.

"I vill instruct you," said Naomi. "I vill show you zee bloodroot," she laughed, backing away as he tried to kiss her again. "I zinc you vill like zat one. It gives zee red juice, vich zee Indians used for var paint . . ." Naomi backed herself right against a birch tree.

With a soft war whoop Danny dropped his walking stick and kissed her again, leaning his palms against the trunk of the tree. She closed her eyes and thought, Danny is kissing me. It still seemed like a miracle. All the time she had listened to Polly talk about boys, shrugging it off as if dating were no big deal, all that time it had seemed like the impossible dream to Naomi. Having a boy want you. Choose you. Danny kissed and kissed her, till she thought she would lose her breath.

"You have little gold crinkles in your eyes," he told her, when at last he lifted his mouth from hers, "just like this." He drew a wiggly circle in the air, making her laugh. His voice slid to a whisper. "Oh, Naomi."

His hands slipped from the tree to her shoulders, and when he kissed her this time he pushed against her till she felt the ridge of the birch's peeling bark against her spine and shoulder blades, even through her thick sweater. He had never kissed her like this before, not even in the back of Donny's car. She felt as if she were losing her balance, as if one leg had suddenly become shorter than the other and she might topple over at any moment. Kissing her, kissing her, she could hardly breathe. Naomi moved her foot; a twig snapped; a crow barked and flew up.

It came to her that she and Danny were completely alone.

"Danny." At last, gently, she pushed him away. She had the uneasy feeling, the way she did when they were around Donny, that he was trying to prove something. "Come on, Danny. We're almost there."

"Where?"

"You'll see. Come on."

She took his hand and he let her lead him farther down the path. Past the clump of hemlock, down the small slope where you had to be careful not to trip over exposed roots, to the edge of the marsh — what in the world? Looming up out of the marsh, its tires sunk in the soft black ooze, was a topless red convertible. Sitting there surrounded by woods it looked like a giant fossil, the lone relic of a former civilization.

"That wasn't here last year!" Naomi cried. "Who'd have been crazy enough to try and drive in here?"

The car's upholstery spit out stuffing and its back seat was full of squashed beer cans. There was a hole in the dashboard where someone had taken out the radio, and little red, yellow, and blue wires dangled down.

"Why would anybody drive in here?" Naomi asked again. "This is no place for cars."

Danny kicked the tires like a man in a used-car lot, tried to pop the hood but found it too rusted. Suddenly he leaped over the front door and into the driver's seat. "Probably some kids out for kicks," he said. "You know these kids today." He grabbed the steering wheel and pretended to drive. "Now when *I* was a boy . . ." When Naomi laughed he gave a wolf whistle. "Hey, little girl, want a ride?"

"Oh no! My mother told me never to take rides with strangers."

"I'll give you candy." He twirled an imaginary mustache. Naomi laughed uneasily. "Come on out of there, Danny. That car gives me the creeps."

"Oh come on, Naomi, don't be a drag. Come and sit in here with me a minute."

Gingerly, Naomi stepped over the mud and climbed into the seat beside him. He put one arm around her and with the other palmed the wheel, making motor sounds. "Rooom, rarooom." Then, as if they were going faster, he began roaring louder and louder. "Errrrrr*rrrr,* errrr*rrrroom!* Rororo-roooom!"

"Danny, you're crazy — you sound just like my little brother playing with his trucks."

Suddenly he flung himself against her as if taking a turn on two wheels. Pretending to swing the steering wheel wildly, "Look out!" he shouted.

"Danny, are you . . ."

"Close one! Oh no, hold on, another hairpin." He pulled her against him.

"You've been watching too much TV!"

"Hang on, little sister!"

"You're making my stomach hurt! I'm getting dizzy! Stop now!"

But Danny didn't stop. He gripped the wheel with one hand and pinned her against him with the other, roaring and squealing and varooming like a car out of control. Now a siren sound . . .

"This isn't really what I had in mind." The silent woods,

bird songs, the two of them among the wildflowers . . .

"Danny, I really mean it!"

"Look out — bustin' glass!"

It began to feel too real, as if she actually were in a speeding car, with Danny flinging her along and no way for her to stop him. Careening along on his whim, all out of her control. Naomi was suddenly frightened.

"Danny, please . . ."

"Hang on!"

"You're scaring me!"

"If we can just make this last curve . . ."

This time he pulled her against him so abruptly she was flung across his chest and wound up half in his lap, half hanging out over the top of the rusty red door.

And that was when she saw them. A dozen or more, rising up like small green sea serpents from the deep black ooze.

"Danny, look!" she cried, chin on the door. "They've been here all the time, and we didn't notice! The skunk cabbage! The first wildflowers, Danny! Danny?"

But Danny was kissing her ear, her neck, her collarbone, Danny had his hand inside her sweater and was touching her breasts, her spine, Danny was suddenly everywhere and Naomi was suddenly lying on her back on the front seat, looking up from underneath at all the little red, yellow, and blue wires dangling down where they weren't supposed to.

"Oh, you feel so nice. You feel so soft, Naomi."

"Polly says I have a Rubenesque figure," she gasped, trying to wriggle up on one elbow.

"Polly Polly Polly, you talk about Polly too much."

What would Polly do in a situation like this? It was hard to think, considering it was taking all her energy to keep from slipping back down onto the seat. "Danny, do you want to talk about cars? Explain internal combustion again? I promise I won't be bored."

"Naomi, don't you like this?"

"No! I mean, yes, but —"

"Don't be afraid."

"Afraid? Who, me? Oh my God, what was that? Someone's coming!"

Danny sat bolt upright. "What? I don't hear anything."

Naomi could have told him she didn't either. Instead, she took the chance to scramble up and over the side of the car. Forgetting about the mud. And that she was not the world's most coordinated person. Landing squat, plop, ugh, in the ocean of ooze. Feet straight out before her, heels sinking in the bubbly goo. Danny's incredulous face peered down at her.

"I've heard of communing with nature," he said, "but aren't you overdoing it?"

"The worst thing was I stunk of skunk," Naomi told Polly during the Instant Replay. "Worse. Dead skunk."

"Sounds romantic."

"Yeah." That wasn't the worst thing at all. The worst thing was that she had tried to blend her two happinesses, and the result had been disaster. She'd thought, What could be more wonderful than sharing my secret with *him*? Wouldn't that be the greatest happiness of all? But Danny didn't even realize how he'd disappointed her. He'd laughed and pulled her up out of the mud and said, "Let's get out of here." Later he said again what a great place it'd be to have a party. Naomi imagined the solemn, silent woods echoing with music and shouting, the ferns and wildflowers trampled, birds traumatized, earth littered with bottles and cans — she squeezed her eyes shut in horror.

"I pointed out to him that he usually stinks of gas and oil, and he had the nerve to say gas and oil smell good."

She waited for Polly to begin her usual lecture: Nome, your desires and your interests are just as valid as his. Just remember that, and if he tries to dominate you, then . . .

Instead, she heard Polly say, her voice very soft, "Maybe they do smell good. To him."

"Polly? Do you feel okay? Did something happen?"

Chapter Seven

As soon as Polly woke up that Saturday, she thought, Something is going to happen.

She lay in bed, the intuition turning her insides to Jell-O, lemon yellow Jell-O. The sunlight danced, trembling, on the walls of her room, and something inside her danced, too, as if the quiver that went through her at the first note of certain songs was caught, vibrating, inside her.

Down the hall she heard Cass singing, " 'But I don't want no part-time lover!' " The front door slammed. Cass was off to her paper route. It had been Polly's route once; she had been the first paper*girl* in the neighborhood. "Collect!" she would say, in as deep a voice as she could manage, her toothpick of a body swallowed up inside the big gray EXPRESS CARRIER sweatshirt. People laughed. They gave her big tips, and she got so many new orders that she won all kinds of prizes — measuring cups that stacked to look like a beehive, an imitation brass eagle to hang on the wall, a badminton set, and once even a twelve-pound frozen turkey, which was nice, since it was the first Thanksgiving after her father left, and there'd been a chance they'd be eating hot dogs instead. When Polly retired she passed the route on to Cass, who just last month won a ten-speed. "You Quinn gals are real go-getters, ain't you?" the paper manager chuckled, chomping his cigar.

The sun had already moved, and now the dancing white light fell on the plant Naomi had given her for her birthday. It was a begonia — *semperflorens,* Naomi said: always blooming. Since her father's long-distance gifts Polly hadn't cared for presents in general, but this one had made her especially uneasy. "Anyone can grow a begonia," Naomi had reassured her. Anyone but Polly, it seemed. The plant stood in its little clay pot, a small brown twig with two papery leaves, and where the flowers had been there were nothing but small brown crumples, like the discarded skins of tiny snakes.

"What's going to happen today?" Polly asked it. "Do you know, my poor beggaronia?"

"Polly? Are you awake? You'll be late for work."

"All right."

Polly got out of bed slowly, trying not to jostle the feeling inside her. She dressed in jeans, a pale blue shirt, and sneakers. She plaited her hair into one thick braid and tied it with a pale blue ribbon. For spring. From her closet she took the pink smock with the big white plastic buttons and WALLY's MARKET stitched in orange on the pocket. The smock should have been hideous but (and she knew this) it suited Polly, the way anything she put on did. Sometimes men who came through her checkout tried to flirt with her, which always made her laugh.

Her mother was sitting at the kitchen table, with a cup of coffee and a cigarette, absently humming "Part-time

Lover." She was dressed in old clothes, and her hair was pulled back in an old chipped barrette of Polly's.

"Slugabed!" she greeted her daughter. "I've been up for hours! It's a glorious day!"

"Is it?" Polly poured herself a glass of orange juice and drank it slowly, standing by the back door.

"It is. I've just come in from yard inspection. That ice storm last month did more damage than I thought. I'm afraid we may lose the Japanese maple, and the hemlock will definitely have to be supported. Is that all you're having for breakfast?"

"How are the lilacs?" They were Polly's favorite.

"Oh, they're fine. You can't kill lilacs. The forsythia has a good deal of winterkill, though. And I'll have to attack those dry wells right away. They're just choked with debris."

Polly opened the door and stuck her head out. The morning was so warm she propped the door open. "Why don't you take a day off?" she asked her mother. "If I didn't have to go to work I'd lie outside all day, doing nothing."

Her mother laughed, stubbing out her cigarette. "There are times, Polly Quinn, I fear I've spoiled you rotten."

"No, really. When Cass gets home you could both hop in the car and go for a long walk on the beach."

Catherine Quinn had a funny smile, tight-lipped, as if she'd swallowed something good and was trying to keep the taste in her mouth. "A habit," she once told Polly, "from when I was your age and ashamed of my teeth." Sitting there smiling now, without any makeup, in her faded plaid shirt and washed-out pants, she looked much younger than she was. It was easy to recognize her as the girl in the 1960 John Jay High School yearbook — Catherine Michaels, Valedictorian, little white lights glinting in her eyes, lips pressed together, a string of pearls glowing softly around her neck.

"You should give yourself a break," Polly said, finishing her orange juice. "Relax." Yet even as she said it she knew it was useless.

"As if there were anything in the world I'd rather do than work in my yard. As if I could relax with my hemlock drooping." Mrs. Quinn drained her coffee and clinked the cup down on the saucer. "Are you about ready? I'll drive you to Wally's."

"I think I'll walk today. It's so beautiful out."

"Well, you better scoot then."

"Bye."

"Goodbye." Mrs. Quinn held out her cheek, and Polly gave her a kiss.

Before she left, Polly took her begonia out into the back yard. She put it on the redwood picnic table, where it looked up at her forlornly from among the fallen twigs and dead maple leaves.

"You get better," Polly whispered to it. "It's spring — time to grow!"

Wally's Market was on the edge of a shopping mall that sprawled out in five directions. A concrete starfish in a sea of asphalt, Polly planned to describe it in her novel. "A checker's job," she told Naomi, "is a slice of life. You see it all — the little old lady with the quarter pound of baloney and cans of cat food, the bleary-eyed young guy nodding over his basket full of Pampers and strained pears, the woman in the fur coat and diamond rings who pays for her one box of macaroni and cheese with pennies. My novel will be a series of quick flashes, like the flipping of a TV dial." Naomi, who had already heard Polly's intentions to be an architect, an astronomer, and a museum curator, nodded politely. But Polly was serious. She took notes for her novel on brown paper bags. Some Saturday mornings it was the only thing that kept her sane.

That morning she arrived at Wally's in a drowsy, dreamy mood. The walk there wasn't exactly scenic — up the highway past one fast-food place and discount store after another — but the air was so gentle, and the soft light seemed to mute the ugliness of the buildings, blur the garish signs. Birds sang on the telephone wires. She caught a whiff of fresh-turned earth.

"Five and a half minutes late — what d'ya think this is, a country club? Well, it comes outa your pay, not mine, honey. You're on Register Three and it's Can Can Day, so if I were you I'd wake up pronto!"

The manager was out and the assistant manager was making sure everyone knew *he,* Mr. Joe Atwater, was in charge. He was only a few years older and not an inch taller than Polly. On his head he wore a little paper cap that said it's A PLEASURE TO SERVE YOU!

Polly gave him the saccharine smile she usually reserved for hall monitors, put on her smock, and took her place behind Register 3. It was right in the middle, the busiest one.

As soon as Joe unlocked the door a crowd of people rushed in, grabbed up carts, and zoomed down the aisles. It was Can Can Day. Everything that came in a can was on sale. Polly had never realized the number and variety of things that came in cans. It was truly astounding. There were clams and hams and jams in cans, tomatoes, potatoes, and something called Puratos, soups made with oxtails, ready-mix cocktails, pudding and sardines, tacos and baked beans — it might have made Polly laugh, if she'd had the time. Which she didn't. Before she'd finished ringing up one customer, the next was stacking his cans on the belt. She had to pick up nearly every can to look at the sale price, and after a while she began to get grooves in her fingertips. Then she had to pack the bags; each one weighed a ton. All around the store were sexist posters of women in cancan costumes; in the produce aisle a motorized woman kicked her black-stockinged leg up and down, up and down, narrowly missing the banana tree. On her mental typewriter Polly tapped out a scene in which the mechanical woman kicked Joe in the head, he staggered backward, an avalanche of tuna cans cascaded down, and thus ended the career of the power-mad Mr. Joe Atwater . . .

"Break time, honey. And let's punch out, okay?"

Punch you out, ha ha.

Polly got two tart green apples, paid for them under Joe's hawk eyes, and escaped out the back of the store, through the big door where the trucks pulled up. It was almost noon and the sun hit her on top of her head, right where she parted her hair; she slipped off the pink smock, pushed up her blue sleeves, and felt the heat on her bare arms. Aaah. The green apple was cold and when she bit into it a little juice dribbled down her chin; she licked it up, quick, like a cat. She stretched, arching her back, raised her arms — what was that exercise she learned in yoga last year?

And then she noticed him.

Someone else was out here, too, sitting on a packing case in the middle of this no-man's-land of squashed cardboard boxes and wilted lettuce leaves. It was Crow, she saw, eating yogurt and watching her. Polly had been in the same class with this boy since fourth grade, but she couldn't remember his real name. It was his nose that had given him his nickname, that and his shock of glossy black hair. Polly had seen and not seen Crow for seven years, the way you can go to the same school year in and year out, but when someone asks you what color the halls are painted, you can't say. He was that kind of person. The only time she remembered him attracting any attention was in fifth grade when he threw up right in the middle of the spring concert, just as they began "Daffy Down Dilly Has Come to Town." Now he worked as a stockboy here, and at school was in her minicourse on personality, but she had never spoken to him.

Till now.

"Hello."

"Hello." There was a book on the crate beside him, upside down so she couldn't see its title. He pushed his wire-rims up on his nose.

"I certainly hope you're keeping an eye on the clock," she said, mock-serious. "Joe's timing all breaks with a stopwatch today."

"Joe? That's Mr. Atwater to you, honey!" It was a perfect imitation of the assistant manager, taking Polly by surprise. She laughed, moved a step closer, and saw his dark eyebrows make a movement like a small bird winging up.

"That creep! He's been on my case all morning! His latest thing is making us all say, 'Thank you for shopping Wally's!' to each customer. As if we cared."

"I think it's that cap he wears, the one that says 'It's a Pleasure to Serve You!' It stops the flow of blood to his brain." Crow stirred the yogurt — strawberry, Polly's favorite — then forgot to eat it. "Today he made me set up a display of tuna in the front of the store, then changed his mind and decided it'd sell better in the bread aisle. Two hundred cans of tuna! I'll never eat the stuff again."

"It'll be a long time before I eat *any*thing that comes out of a can again." She showed him her red fingertips and watched as, above his glasses, his brows made that movement again, a bird surprised. "I'm going to dream cans of mixed vegetables are after me. I hated vegetables before, but now I really hate them."

He looked at her seriously. "I bet you've never had fresh-picked vegetables. Fresh-picked peas are like candy."

Polly grinned. His sudden seriousness reminded her of Cass, who could be so solemn about the littlest thing. "That's hard to believe."

"It's true." Abruptly he tilted back the yogurt carton and drank the rest down. Polly watched him wipe his chin on the back of his hand and crush the empty carton in his fist. "I guess I better be going back in."

"Before Numero Uno comes out after you."

He picked up his book. "Well. See you, Polly."

"See you."

He disappeared back into the store.

Polly took one last bite of her apple and threw the core in the trash. She stood tossing the other one up, catching it, tossing it up. It made a nice round sound when it fell into her hands. What was Crow's real name? He knew her name, all right. The Jell-O feeling came over her again. Crazy. Spring fever. When she went back in she gave Joe Atwater such a wide, friendly smile he looked at her suspiciously.

Several hours later she walked back home, back down the highway, where the birds had abandoned the telephone wires for secret hollows in the still-bare trees. At home, eight plastic leaf bags were lined up neatly beside the garage. Cass was turning cartwheels in the back yard, and Polly turned one, two, three in a row. Then she picked up her begonia, and carefully carried it back to her room.

Chapter Eight

That Monday in Personality Polly sat next to Boom Boom Bottzemeyer and diagonally across the circle of desks from Crow. Crow had a sunburn. When he took off his glasses she saw the little strip of pale skin across the bridge of his nose. He didn't look back at her; while Mr. Haight lectured he stared up at the ceiling. Boom Boom drew pictures of Mr. Haight's bald head, trying to make her laugh.

"The Compensator," Mr. Haight wrote on the board, and turned to face the class. "This is the person who is continually making amends for some felt defect. Take, for instance, the short man who feels he must continually assert his authority to make up for his lack of height, who has to prove over and over again that he's a man, capital M, no matter how small he is."

Crow's gaze toppled from the ceiling, directly into Polly's eyes. Mr. Joe Atwater, of course. He was no taller than she was.

Polly waited for Crow after class.

"Maybe if we bought Joe a pair of elevator shoes he'd leave us alone," he said.

"Poor Joe. Mighty Midget. Maybe if we started crouching down when he talks to us?"

Crow's chest was sunburned, too, the little V where the skin showed inside his shirt. The cover of his Personality book was doodled all over with intersecting lines labeled with words Polly couldn't make out. He was also carrying the same paperback she'd seen him with in Wally's lot.

"That must be a good book," she said, tapping it.

"Oh, phh." He looked embarrassed. Then, abruptly, he held it up for her to see.

"The Complete Guide to Vegetable Growing?"

He nodded. "I'm planting a garden. I never did it before."

"Oh." Images of leaf bags and piles of wilting weeds rose in Polly's mind. Bor-r-r-ring. "I've never been very good at growing things. My friend gave me a begonia for my birthday. She said anyone could grow a begonia. But I'm afraid I've killed mine."

Standing by her locker he showed her the doodled cover of his Personality book. "See, certain things grow better when they're planted together. They call it companion planting. Like, if you put basil among the tomatoes, it keeps certain bugs away. Or you can plant lettuce among the sweet corn, because lettuce likes shade." He showed her all the different sketches he had made, trying to find the ideal plan for his garden. His hair fell across his glasses and he had that solemnity again, that unselfconscious gravity that made her smile.

He fiddled with the catch on her locker. "Maybe you could come see it sometime," he said. "Maybe today? I'm planting the peas today."

Polly had to catch herself before she laughed. Boys had asked her to chess tournaments, circuses, bar mitzvahs, poetry readings, wrestling meets, second cousins' weddings, and parties held everywhere from the Starduster to deserted houses (Polly had been dating since sixth grade), but she had never before been invited to a pea planting.

Before she could answer, Boom Boom Bottzemeyer appeared, waving a daffodil in one hand. He was so tall that when Polly danced with him she could lay her head right on his heart. If she felt like it. Boom Boom had sleepy blue eyes and hair the color of vanilla fudge. He was wearing a dark beret and bouncing on the toes of his sneakers as if he'd just made a touchdown.

"I snatched this off Armbruster's desk," he said, grinning

and waving the daffodil at Polly. Armbruster: Polly's arch-enemy, the Home Ec teacher who once, in front of the whole class, had made Polly rip the pocket off her sewing project. "This pocket is a disgrace!" Armbruster said, and Polly calmly replied that in this day and age forcing girls to make aprons was the real disgrace. For that moment of truth she'd gotten a week's detention.

"I thought how much better it would look in your hair than on her mangy desk," Boom Boom told Polly, and reached over and slipped the flower behind her ear. For such a big guy he wasn't at all clumsy with his hands. "There."

"Thanks, Boom," said Polly, twirling the combination on her lock. "Though next time you might try buying me a flower, instead of stealing it." She opened her locker door, but Boom Boom's big shoulder came against it and thumped it shut.

"Hey," he said, ducking his head and lowering his voice. "Hey, kid, don't you have something to tell me?" He was the only guy Polly had ever met who could imitate Bogart and get away with it. "What's the verdict on going to the prom with me?"

"The evidence isn't all in yet." She jerked open her locker door, banging him on the shoulder. He gave his Bogie chuckle.

"I don't know about you, Quinn," he said, in a way that implied he knew a *lot* about her. "You like to play Ms. Cool, but . . ."

The bell rang and Polly slammed her locker. "Sorry, Boom, I don't have time to be psychoanalyzed right now. Maybe Friday, at Tom's party."

"We'll see about that. Catch you later." He loped off down the hall.

Polly turned back to Crow, and he was gone. She caught

sight of him at the opposite end of the hall, halfway up the stairs. "Crow! Crow! Sorry about that," she said, catching up to him. "Boom Boom's part bulldozer—he just pushes over whatever's in his way."

"That's okay." Crow looked at the daffodil in her hair. "I have to go. I have Lee, and you know how he is about being late . . ."

"Crow, can I come see your garden this afternoon?"

He stood stock-still for a moment, and then his face broke into a smile. A faceful of smile. "Sure," he said. "Sure. I'll come to your locker—or do you want to come to my locker? Sure!" He took the rest of the steps two at a time, then suddenly stopped and leaned over the railing. Looking down at her, "My name's Jonathon," he said.

"Okay, Jonathon."

"Okay! Sure!"

Polly slipped into the cafeteria ten minutes late without getting caught, and found Naomi just coming out of the lunch line. Her tray held pizza, French fries, and two ice-cream sandwiches.

"Thank God Danny doesn't have lunch this period. I promised him I'd start my diet today."

"Guess where I'm going? To see Crow's garden."

Naomi's mouth made a shape like an egg. "Crow? A garden? I thought you thought gardening was boring."

"I do. It is. But he asked me, and . . ."

Naomi's face lit up. "So, do you do everything Crow asks you to do?"

Polly made a face at her and stole one of her French fries. "Jonathon. His name is Jonathon. I don't know, I guess it's because he seemed so vulnerable." She licked her fingers, thoughtfully ran her knuckle over the bump in her nose.

"It seemed like if I said, 'To tell you the truth, Crow, I'm not at all interested in your peas,' he'd just have crumpled up. Like cellophane when you throw it in the fire." She ate another French fry. "He almost reminds me of Cass — very vulnerable, underneath."

Naomi held a French fry up before her face. "Sixteen calories each," she sighed, and swallowed it down. "Danny talked me into going to see *The Faceless* this weekend. He keeps saying what a good time we're going to have. He says it like this." Naomi wiggled her eyebrows. *"What* a good time."

"Let me teach you a few karate chops."

"Oh, I'm not really worried," said Naomi with a worried frown. She contemplated another fry. "Sometimes I wish there was no such thing as s-e-x. Or that I was born a hundred years ago, when it wasn't such a big thing. I mean, Danny and I could be such good friends, if only it wasn't for *that.* I know that means I'm repressed and neurotic." She sighed again, wolfed down the rest of the fries. "Hey, where'd you get that daffodil?"

"Old Boom Boom — otherwise known as Sticky Fingers — Bottzemeyer." Polly pulled it out from behind her ear. "Here, do you want it?"

"Danny would get jealous. I hope."

Polly shrugged and tossed it onto Naomi's tray, where it landed in the ketchup. "He should know by now I don't like presents."

Naomi sighed and began on her pizza. No one had ever given her a flower. No one but her parents when she turned "sweet" sixteen, and you could hardly count that.

Chapter Nine

✿ "We can walk to my house," Crow told her when they met that afternoon.

"All right."

It was a long walk, and somewhere along the way they crossed one of those invisible boundaries that divide "good" from "bad" neighborhoods. The yards began to shrink; the paint on the houses began to flake; litter appeared in the gutters or stuck between the slats of fences.

"This is my street. I better warn you about my house. Last night I was brushing my teeth, and the whole place started to shake."

The street was lined with two-family houses. Shoulder to shoulder, like people on a crowded bus, the houses formed a wall along each side of the street. Polly thought that could make you feel secure or claustrophobic, depending. The street was full of shrieking, just-let-out-of-prison schoolchildren, barking dogs, and paper whirling in the wind. Polly had the strange feeling she'd been here before, but she knew that couldn't be.

"We live downstairs." Crow unlocked his door and they stepped into a long hall lit by a single bulb on the ceiling. Rooms opened off the hall like compartments off a train corridor. "No one's here. My father's at work."

"And you leave the light on? What a waste of energy." Polly snapped it off.

He led her down the hall, into a small yellow kitchen that was like the light at the end of a tunnel, and out the back door. The whole back yard, from one chain-link fence to the other, was raw earth.

"You're really serious about this, aren't you?" she said.

"I'm not even sure anything will grow out here. The soil seems pretty bad. But I took a sample to the Farm and Garden Bureau, and they said . . ."

He explained all about pH and acidity, nitrogen and lime. A walking course in earth science, he moved around his garden plucking up a rusty bottle cap here, a few stones there. The cuffs of his jeans got caked with mud, he smeared earth on his forehead when he brushed back that lock of hair, but he didn't seem to notice. Polly smiled to herself, trying to see what he saw, what he was getting so excited over. It looked like a patch of dirt to her.

All at once he stopped his pacing and said, "I'm compensating."

"You're what?"

"You know, like Joe Atwater does for being short. I'm compensating for my rootless childhood." He grinned, as if to let her take it as a joke, but he went on, "My father and I've lived all over town, renting here and there. This is the first place we ever had a yard, and something made me want to have a garden. You know, put down roots for real."

She sat in the rusting metal chair by the back door. "Just you and your father?"

He reached for the shovel leaning against the house. "My mother's dead."

"Oh." She picked at the chair's peeling white paint. "I didn't —"

"She died when I was three."

"Three is little."

He drove the shovel into the earth and leaned his weight on it. "Yeah. . . . Well, you know what it's like, some. I mean your father — I know about that."

"I guess everybody knows about that."

"I remember when we were in fourth grade, some kids teasing you out in the play yard. They were croaking like parrots and saying, 'Polly want a father? Polly want a papa?'"

Polly picked at the chair's paint. "You remember that?"

"I wanted to kill those kids."

She looked up. "So did I."

"I remember you kicked Boom Boom Bottzemeyer in the stomach. I couldn't believe it — he could have creamed you, just by sitting on you! He was so fat then. He was teasing you the worst of all."

"I told you he had no manners." She smiled.

"I'd wanted to do the same thing for a long time. Kick him, I mean. He used to ride my bus when we lived on Cannon Street, and every time I got on he'd hold his nose and double over and everybody would howl."

"He was an awful bully. He used to tease everybody."

"Compensating for being fat."

They both laughed. "I'll have to tell him that," said Polly.

"I guess you know him pretty well."

Polly shrugged. "I'm not tempted to kick him in the stomach anymore, if that's what you mean."

"Once my father got me a crew cut and for a week Bottzemeyer had everyone calling me 'skinhead.'"

"No wonder you wanted to kill him that day in the school yard."

Crow brushed his hair out of his eyes, smearing a little more dirt on his forehead. "No," he said. "It was because he was hurting you."

"Oh, but he didn't." Polly sat up straight in her chair. "I got him so hard, I thought he'd deflate and go spinning around the yard like a punctured balloon. I remember, I was wearing brown-and-white saddle shoes. I hated them, but my mother said they were good for my feet. Bam, I got him!" She struck her palm with her fist. "I was so disappointed when all he did was sit down and cry."

"You cried, too."

"No."

"That's how I remember it."

"I thought we were going to plant some peas."

"Right."

On one edge of the garden he drew a perfectly straight line with the shovel handle, then made a little trench along it. When he was satisfied that all the clods of dirt were broken up, and every stone removed, he shook some seeds, the ghosts of former peas, into her hand. Side by side, Polly and Crow went along the trench, dropping in the seeds and crumbling the soft earth over them.

"There," he said. "Now they're your peas, too."

"I hate peas," she said, standing up and brushing the dirt off her knees.

"You'll like these."

Chapter Ten

Overnight the weather turned cold again, the puddles growing mother-of-pearl skins, the soft, squishing earth hardening into a crust. That was all right, Crow told Polly. There were still lots of things they could plant. "As soon as the ground can be worked," it said on the backs of the seed packages spread on his kitchen table: peas, beets, carrots, cabbage, parsley, radishes, lettuce. Crow had sent away for the seeds and now Polly picked them up and read their names out loud. "Buttercrunch, Egyptian Wonder, Blue Bantam, Ruby Queen, Stonehead. Stonehead?"

"Today we plant chard."

"Charred?"

"Chard. It's like spinach. To make us strong to the finish, like Popeye."

"I hate vegetables."

It was Thursday; she had been there every day that week. A drizzle began to fall as they worked, and Polly retreated to the kitchen long before the last chard seed was in. When Crow came in at last, his glasses steaming and his hair pearled with raindrops, she attacked him with a dish towel.

"Yow!"

"Do you want to catch pneumonia?" she demanded, rubbing his head.

"Do you want me bald at the age of sixteen?"

"Hold still now! Remember when you were little and stayed out sleigh riding or skating till you were blue, and your mother would grab you up and rub you like this — you'd yell, 'Yow!' — but afterwards you felt so warm —"

Too late she bit her tongue. Of course Crow couldn't have memories like that.

"I had a babysitter who did that." His face was rosy; he straightened his glasses on his nose. "When I yelled she'd say, 'Pain is good. When you hurt you know you're alive.' My father called her the Croaker but I kind of liked her. She always smelled like Vicks Vaporub."

"Huh." Polly neatly folded the towel over the back of a chair.

"I think I used to half hope my father'd marry her." Crow put a pot of water on and spooned instant coffee into two cups.

"It's good you don't mind talking about your mother."

He turned. "I do mind. Usually."

"If there's one thing I hate it's when people talk about my father in hushed voices, as if we had some fatal disease. Leprosy. Things happen, life goes on, that's how it is. It's no use feeling sorry for yourself." Polly tossed her hair. "He left so long ago, it's almost like he was never there."

He put a can of evaporated milk and a box of sugar doughnuts on the table. "I'd think you'd be mad."

"Mad?"

"At him, for leaving you."

"What good would that do?"

"Not much, I guess. I just remember, when I was small, some nights I used to lie in bed and hate my mother for dying."

The water boiled over, and Polly jumped up. Stirring the coffee, her back to Crow, "But that was when you were small," she said.

"I still remember how it feels to be small. Don't you?"

She carefully carried the brimful cups to the table. They sat across from each other, blowing on the hot coffee. Crow's glasses steamed up again when he took a sip. It began to rain harder; they could hear it drumming on the metal chair outside. Rain blurred the windows, wrapped them in a silvery cocoon. Polly watched him break a sugar doughnut in half, his fingertips turning powdery white. He put one half on her plate. Inside it was gold.

"I don't like to remember being small," she said. "People who get all sentimental over childhood have forgotten what it was really like." The tires of a passing car hissed on the wet street. She stirred her coffee, then laughed softly. "How come I keep remembering the past when I'm with you?"

"I don't know."

"Coffee tastes good with evaporated milk. I never had it before."

"My father's always used it. See how the can has a picture of the can on it? And the picture of the can has a picture of a can? When I was little, I used to stare and stare at it, thinking how it could go on and on forever like that, getting smaller and smaller. It really spaced me out."

"I still feel like that, when I think about the stars."

He told her about his father, who managed a movie theater. She told him about the foreign films they showed for a dollar over at the community college, and how much better they were than most American films. Crow said he'd never seen a foreign film.

"You should expand your horizons."

"You sound like your mother."

"How do you—"

"I had her in seventh grade. I was in your friend's class. Naomi."

Before Polly left she peered out the window at the garden. Bare earth, with little sticks and brightly colored seed packages marking the rows. Pictures of carrots, chard, beets, peas —they looked so hopeful, even with the rain beating on them. Still, it was hard to believe anything was going on out there. Polly had trouble believing in things she couldn't see.

"Just be patient," Crow told her. "The peas will be the first thing."

He lent her his father's umbrella, a huge black thing with one bent spoke, and came out with her to the street. She walked to the corner slowly, stepping over bits of glass and puddles full of drowned worms, knowing he was watching her. At the corner she turned and waved. Leaning on the rickety fence there in the rain he gave a little start, embarrassed at being caught, and then waved back.

At home she began a new chapter in her supermarket novel: "Among the aisles of plastic plants and freeze-dried-micro-waved-plastic-wrapped-synthetic-instant foods, he dreamed of something more pure." Too corny. Polly pulled the paper out of the typewriter and crumpled it into a ball. She stared at Naomi's begonia and remembered Crow's face when they planted the chard. What was that word he used? Gentle. You have to be gentle with these growing things, he said. She thought of the shape his lips made, saying that.

Chapter Eleven

Polly didn't go to Crow's the next afternoon. When she told him she had to go straight home after school he said, "Sure," as if he'd been expecting her to say that sooner or later. He looked so crushed — the cellophane in the fire — that Polly almost said, "Well, all right, I'll come for a little while, then." But she decided that was ridiculous. It was his garden, after all. She had previous commitments.

"I'll call you for Instant Replay as soon as I get home from the party," she told Naomi, who was going to see *The Faceless* with Danny. And Donny. "Good luck."

Naomi rolled her eyes.

At home Polly washed her hair and laid out the clothes

� 55 🌿

she would wear to Tom DeMillo's party. She chose them carefully — a long flowered skirt, a leotard, the satin-backed vest — knowing how important looks were to old Boom Boom. One reason he liked going out with her was that she always stood out in a group, always turned heads. Boom Boom was so conscious of his image, he made her laugh. His thing was hats. He had an enormous collection, and he changed his personality to suit each one. For his yearbook photo, as Mr. Sully, he had posed in a top hat. "When you lost your baby fat," Polly liked to tease him, "you replaced it with a fat ego. You act like you invented the wheel. Discovered fire." Boom Boom would tip his hat over his eyes. "Look out you don't get burned, Ms. Cool."

Polly stood before her mirror, twisting her hair into tiny braids. Our conversations are like party favors, she thought, the ones we used to get at birthday parties. We'd blow into them and unfurl a little tunnel of pretty-colored paper. We'd shoot them into each other's faces — that's what our conversations are like. Little taunts, quick digs — we shoot them at each other and then we roll them right back up before we can look at them too closely. Old 3B. He'll be the life of Tom's party. *Life* is a party, for him. He's the perfect person to go with.

Then why don't I feel like going with him?

— What, you don't want to go to Tom DeMillo's party? People have been talking about it for weeks, ever since Tom's parents decided to go on that cruise!

I know. Maybe I looked forward to it too much. You can spoil things, you know, by too much anticipation. It's better to be surprised.

— You're crazy. It's not that.

Well, maybe it's just this rain and cold, after those warm, beautiful days. It's depressing.

—You're making excuses.

Polly began to pin the braids up on top of her head. It took her so long to find an arrangement that pleased her, her arms began to ache, and her neck to feel stiff. Maybe I'm getting the flu. The aches and pains of flu. Boom Boom, I'm sorry, but I have to rest in bed, drink plenty of fluids, and take Bayer . . .

From down the hall came a peal of Cass's laughter. "What's the matter—you got a pain in the neck?" she asked when Polly appeared in the kitchen doorway, holding her head erect.

On the table was the big blue bowl that had once belonged to Catherine Quinn's mother. It was full of cream-colored dough, studded with raisins and nuts and flecked with sweet brown spice.

"Hot cross buns, hot cross buns, if you have no daughters, give them to your sons!" sang Mrs. Quinn, breaking off a piece of the dough and patting it into a small round loaf.

"You got daughters," admonished Cass, sneaking a bit of dough into her mouth.

"I *have* daughters, thank you, and don't eat that raw dough or it will swell up inside you and make your stomach look like a watermelon."

"Oh sure, Mommy."

"Did you come to help us bake, Polly?"

"It's Lent already? I didn't even know." Polly took a piece of the soft, warm dough and rolled it between her palms. The Quinns didn't go to church. They used to, but religiousness had fallen off with Mr. Quinn's parcel-post presents. "Wants to prove she doesn't need God any more than she needs a man," Polly had once overheard some old biddy mutter about Catherine. Polly understood her mother's trouble with God. He—or She—was one of those things, like the embryo plants in Crow's garden, you couldn't see. But still, every Lent Mrs. Quinn got out her blue bowl and they made hot cross buns; every Easter it was kulich; every Christmas, stollen; for Epiphany they made almond cake, and for St. Pat's Day there was always Irish soda bread. "Traditions are important," Mrs. Quinn would quote in her teacher voice, getting out the blue bowl, the creased and spotted recipes. "Traditions keep the wolf of insignificance from the door."

They ate supper in the kitchen, the buns baking, steaming up the windows and filling the air with spicy sweetness. Mrs. Quinn was in a good mood; she talked about how this spring she meant to paint the garage, put in another azalea, and repaper the kitchen. "Feathering our nest," she called it. They ate the hot cross buns hot, the butter melting in white-gold rivulets, and Cass said, "I feel cozy." Looking around the room, Polly thought of Crow's gloomy kitchen, and the pang she felt startled her with its intensity.

"Polly, look what time it's gotten to be. Didn't you say your Mr. Bottzemeyer was coming at eight?"

Polly dragged herself down the hall to her room. She turned on the radio, hoping to get into a party mood.

> *She says she's keepin' her heart free,*
> *But I know it's just emp-ty*
> *I don't want no part-time lover.*

I ate too many hot cross buns. My stomach hurts. Maybe it's another flu symptom. And listen to the rain. I probably shouldn't go out. I may get really sick.

— You must be already, if you'd miss Tom's party.

The doorbell rang. Polly slipped thin gold hoops strung with turquoise through her ears, and went into the living room, where she was greeted by Cass's foot in her stomach.

Cass was turning a cartwheel because Boom Boom had brought her a cleat. It was a very big thing in the fourth grade then, wearing a boy's football cleat on a chain around your neck. The preferred thing, of course, was having a boyfriend who actually gave you one, but barring that any old boy's cleat was better than none.

Looking at Boom Boom now, no one could have guessed he knew a football from a can of paint. Tonight he was wearing his Irish wool hat, which he doffed to Mrs. Quinn. He was also wearing a dark wool vest and tweed jacket, and with his tangle of pale curls and unlit pipe looked like a photograph on the back of a book of poetry. Tonight he was obviously doing the Intellectual. While Polly got her coat, he chatted with Mrs. Quinn about how much he was enjoying *Romeo and Juliet,* which he was reading in English class.

"That Juliet, with her fiery imagination and her iron will — I find her one of the most arresting and dynamic women in all of Shakespeare."

Polly gave a loud cough. It was a direct quote, of course, from his English teacher. He probably hadn't even read the play. Still, she had to give him credit — he was the one boy she'd ever brought home who could say more than three words to her mother without stuttering.

"Well, Mr. Bottzemeyer, I hope you pursue this new literary enthusiasm of yours."

"I intend to, Mrs. Quinn."

"Let's go, Boob. I mean Boom."

"Shanks again!" (Cass with a mouthful of hot cross bun.)

Boom Boom's father sold used cars and let his son borrow the big gas guzzlers his lot was full of these days. Boom Boom flipped a dial on the imitation wood dash and Beethoven filled the air.

"Have you ever considered a career on the stage, Boom?"

He reached out and tapped her shoulder. "Why are you sitting ten miles away?"

"I think I'm getting a cold. Maybe even the flu. I'm probably highly contagious, as a matter of fact."

"A party can cure anything."

At Tom DeMillo's, cars jammed the big circular driveway and lined both sides of the street. Every light in the house was on, plus the outdoor floodlights.

"What is he expecting, the Concorde to land?"

"This is going to be some party!"

Tom had taken the precaution of carrying his parents' good lamps, exotic plants, and the collection of porcelain they had brought back from their many trips, upstairs out of the way, and it was a good thing, because the party was already a little wild. Tom himself, his eyes red and his frizzy hair looking like a dandelion gone to seed, was standing on the kitchen table telling anyone who'd listen what a wild and crazy guy he was.

The party didn't really begin, though, till Boom Boom arrived. A magnet, he stood in one corner of the room, leaning against a bookcase, and let people come to him, Mr. Sully, the celebrity in the receiving line. The music was so loud that even though she stood right next to him Polly couldn't hear a word he said. The Intellectual, she saw, held himself slightly above and apart from the party. She watched him bend his head and nod wisely, like a father. Oh yes, my boy — I remember when I, too, was as young, simple, and untutored as you! He had one hand on her shoulder, the one holding the still-unlit pipe, and a paper cup in the other. Whenever a slow song came on, they danced. Tonight anything other than a slow dance was beneath his dignity. While he danced he sang into her ear. Over his shoulder Polly could see Marcia Melon, who had come alone, watching them.

"Is something wrong, babe? You seem out of it tonight."

"You noticed."

"Hey, did I do something wrong?"

"I'm tired of being one of your props, like your hat and your tweeds and your pipe."

"What?" Some maniac had turned up the stereo louder yet.

"I shouldn't have come," she shouted. "I'm not in the mood!"

"Here, have some vitamin C." He handed her a paper cup of warm vodka and orange juice, and she took a few sips. But it didn't help.

Now Tom DeMillo was lying on the rug, imitating, he said, a horseshoe crab. Polly felt herself sinking. Potato chips crunched beneath her foot. Her mouth ached from smiling, and her neck from trying not to muss her hair. She was just about to say, "Let's go," when a slow dance came on and Boom Boom put his arms around her. He held her close, singing into her ear, as if sure that would cure whatever ailed her.

Marcia Melon, small and blond, in a gauze shirt and jeans so tight you could tell she had a quarter in her back pocket, sat in a corner staring at Boom Boom. Polly knew Marcia'd give anything to be in her place, to be dancing with Mr. Sully, Mr. Poet Laureate, Mr. Whoever He Was. Instead of me, Ms. Whoever I Am. That little bit of vodka went to my head. Or maybe it's having my hair twisted up like this. It's stopping the flow of blood to my brain.

"Boom, I—"

"This party's played out," he announced. "Let's go." Bang, the party was over. "We're going to the Hideaway."

Just like that, everyone was heading out the door, crowding into cars, everyone including Tom DeMillo, who tumbled into the back seat of Boom Boom's car leaving all the house lights blazing, the stereo still blaring, the party going on without any people.

At the Hideaway, Naomi and Danny were sitting in a booth beneath a life-size plastic fish with a long shining snout and one beady glass eye. Boom Boom and Polly paused at their table just as Danny was giving the waitress his order.

"Two Seven and Sevens."

"Proof?"

Danny slapped his pockets. "What do you know, I must have left it home."

"I've heard that one before," said the waitress with a yawn. "How about two Cokes, sport?"

Boom Boom, grinning, stretched one arm along the back of the booth. He was a year older than Danny, a man of the world, permitted to drink in public, to drive at night — light-years ahead of poor Danny, who still had to bear the insults of waitresses and beg rides from his big brother. Boom Boom pulled the brim of his wool hat down over one eye.

"You ought to go to the Bourbon Barrel," he counseled Danny. "They serve third-graders there."

"Oh, but we have to go wherever Donny goes," said Naomi, pointing toward the back table where Donny sat with his girlfriend of the doorknob mentality. As soon as Naomi spoke she began to blush. She always blushed around Boom Boom, who, leaning over her and grinning, suddenly looked to Polly like a close relation of the sailfish hanging on the wall.

"That's too bad," he said. "Two's company. You're looking good tonight, Naomi."

Scarlet, crimson, Indian red, magenta — crayon colors from her neck to the roots of her hair. Poor Nome. As if Boom didn't say that to all the girls.

"Thanks," stammered Naomi. "Polly helped me make this jumper." It was dark blue, Danny's favorite color, printed with lighter blue flowers, and cut full and wide so she almost looked slender in it. "Actually Polly just about made the whole thing. I'm not very good at sewing."

"Bread baking, that's more your thing," said Polly. "I'm going to teach you that next. It's a very instinctive thing, not at all like sewing. You'll like it, seeing as you're such an instinctive person. I just made some hot cross —"

"Is that true?" interrupted Danny, turning to Naomi. "Is it true you're an instinctive person?"

Just then the waitress brought the two Cokes, and Naomi reached for hers quickly, peeling her elbow off the sticky table. "Never mind," she said, and if it was possible blushed even harder.

Danny drained half his soda in one swallow. "Hey, you guys should go see *The Faceless*. It's —"

"Awful," said Naomi.

"It's great. It's a remake of an old film. See, there's this scientist who's been experimenting on his daughter, only things went wrong, and she's been reduced to nothing but a pair of *eyes* —"

"Ugh, don't talk about it!" Naomi covered her own eyes.

"He goes around kidnapping all these beautiful girls, trying to get back a face for his daughter. You should see the girls, Boom."

"Sounds sexist to me," said Polly.

"Yeah, I guess it is." Danny grinned. "Anyway, there's this one scene —"

"Boom, you gonna order or no?" Tom DeMillo called from the corner table the rest of the party had crowded around. The waitress stood, impatiently tapping her pen on her pad.

"Catch you later." With a tip of his hat Boom Boom took

Polly's hand, and they went to the seats Tom had saved them by the window.

Danny finished his soda in one more gulp, then went back to where his brother was sitting. Polly watched Naomi pull on her coat slowly, reluctantly, the same way she pulled on her gym clothes, postponing as long as possible the moment when she'd have to start doing jumping jacks, or swatting at a hockey puck. Poor Nome. When would she ever learn to say no? Polly watched her go out the door with Danny, who jangled the keys to his brother's car.

She says she's keepin' her heart free . . .

Someone had put the number-one song on the jukebox. Boom Boom was drinking Irish coffee and nodding condescendingly as Tom DeMillo, his eyes redder and his hair frizzier than ever, told about the time he dropped acid and went rock climbing. Beside her Polly could feel Boom Boom waiting, not really listening to the story, just waiting till he could get his chance to tell an even better one and steal the show. She looked out the window. The rain had let up. In the back seat of Donny's car Danny and Naomi were kissing, when all of a sudden the two heads disappeared, *whoosh,* like puppets in a Punch and Judy show.

"I have a headache," said Polly.

But I know it's just emp-ty . . .

"Boom, is it true fresh-picked peas taste like candy?"

He looked at her somberly, felt her forehead for fever. "Something tells me it's time to take you home."

They got out to the parking lot just in time to see Donny tapping on the window of his car, the Doorknob clutching his arm and giggling.

"Anybody home? Break it up in there!"

Polly considered going over and kicking him in the shin, but decided that would embarrass Naomi even more.

The lamp set in the exact center of the Quinns' picture window cast a gold rectangle on the dark front lawn. Boom Boom kissed Polly once in the car and then walked her, holding her arm, to her front door. He was very careful with her, the doctor and the invalid. He kissed her once more in the gray shadows of the front steps, told her to take two aspirin, and said he would call her tomorrow to see how she was.

Mrs. Quinn was already in bed. Polly tiptoed into her own room, sat on the bed, and dialed Naomi's number. Naomi picked it up almost before it rang.

"Polly?" She sounded forlorn and far away. "I didn't think you'd be home so early."

"I think something's the matter with me. I feel rotten."

Naomi sighed. "Me, too. It was one more scene from Big Time Wrestling."

"I know. I could see out the window."

"You could? Oh God. What'd you have to tell me that for? Now I really feel like a fool."

"Well, I couldn't really *see*. I just saw you . . . go under. And not come up."

"I was never so glad to see Donny in my life."

"Being used, Nome. It's the worst."

"I'm just not ready. I look in the mirror and I say, 'Body, are you ready?' And it says, 'Sorry, but not really.'"

"I had this weird feeling tonight, Nome. It was like I was doing a jigsaw puzzle, and all I needed was one more piece. But the piece I had didn't fit. Like I was doing a puzzle of a seashore and was holding a corner of a barn."

"I think I know what you mean."

The two friends sat together a little longer, each in her own dark house, and then they said good night. That night Naomi dreamed that she was drowning, and all the time she struggled for breath a beady-eyed sailfish was watching, waiting to devour her. Polly dreamed she was onstage, in the starring role of a play hundreds and hundreds of people had come to see. She opened her mouth — and discovered she had completely forgotten her lines.

Chapter Twelve

The next morning it was raining again, Polly's hair smelled like cigarette smoke, she still had a headache, and the last thing in the world she felt like doing was going to work at Wally's.

To make matters worse, the regular manager was still out, and Joe Atwater was in charge again. Drunk with power, he assembled what he had begun to call his "crew." Leaning against the wall with her eyes shut, Polly listened to his speech.

"Okay, crew, Mr. Madison is laid up with a bad back and won't be in for a few weeks yet. So the situation is this: I'm in charge, and there are going to be some changes made while I'm running this ship. Now I want you all to listen up, and listen tight." He had definitely seen too many World War II movies. Wearing the little paper cap, he jabbed the air with his pinky, on which he wore a ring with a mammoth red stone.

"All you checkers, and I mean all —" he pointed, for some reason, right at Polly "— you see each and every customer gets a big happy smile and a 'Thank you for shopping Wally's!' After they pay. Understand? I want to hear those thank-you's singing out bright and clear from all, and I mean all, the registers, got it? You, Sleeping Beauty, got it?"

Polly jerked her eyes open. "Got it!" She jabbed her own pinky right back at him.

Behind Joe Atwater Crow laughed out loud, and Joe sputtered, "All right, all right, man your registers!"

It was another hectic morning. The rain, a steady, bone-chilling March rain, put people in a rotten mood. As Polly rang up milk and flour and butter that cost three, four, even ten cents more than they had last week, customers grumbled and complained as if inflation were her fault. One woman paid for her food with eight dollars and thirty-seven cents' worth of change, and Polly had to stand and count it while the line of customers in damp coats and wet shoes stretched all the way to the cookie aisle. Her headache got worse. "You can't buy beer with food stamps," she told a man who refused to believe her. Joe Atwater had to come and say she was right, and both men turned to glare at her. Every now and then she caught a glimpse of Crow, his hair as wet as if he'd been swimming, his wire-rims all steamed up, wheeling in the carts people left in the parking lot. And through it all she kept saying, "Thank you for shopping Wally's!" Through her teeth.

She took her break alone, sitting on a case of beer and eating a strawberry yogurt. Back at her register she couldn't believe the day was only half over. She decided her novel would end with Joe Atwater being clobbered with a leg of frozen lamb. No, better yet, with Joe Atwater as the checker on Register 3.

"Thank you for shopping Wally's!" she said. "Yank you for whopping Wally's."

She said it for what seemed the millionth time — and this

time it came out in stereo. Someone else had said it right along with her. She looked down to the end of her counter and there was Crow, packing for her. From then on they chorused their thanks together. People looked at them as if they were crazy, and then began to smile. Polly's and Crow's voices got louder and louder every time they said it. "Thank you for shopping Wally's. *Thank you for shopping Wally's!*" Before long they were shouting their thanks, bellowing with gratitude, and people were laughing and Joe Atwater was pacing back and forth, smiling at the customers from one side of his face, darting Crow and Polly nasty looks out the other.

All the rest of the afternoon, while Polly tapped at the register, made change, and sent apples, spices, pears, and chocolate down to Crow, all that time she knew something was happening. Inside her something was falling, falling a sweet distance.

He dawdled beside the time clock. She wore her second-hand beaver coat, her pink smock draped over her arm, and he wore a red down jacket. They went outside together. The rain had stopped and the sky was the color of eggshells. A pale, watery sun was trying to break through. Crow's hair was still damp, and as they crossed the parking lot, hopping puddles, he gave a sneeze.

Polly said, "If you get a cold, send Joe your doctor bills."

Crow sneezed again.

"Here, take my hat," she said, pulling it out of her pocket. Crow tried to put it on but it didn't fit. It stood up on his head like a chef's hat, making Polly laugh. He pulled it off and looked at it.

"It's a nice hat."

"I made it."

Crow sneezed again.

"I bet you are getting a cold! That Atwater's a real jerk!"

Crow spread his fingers. "Somebody's got to do his job. You have to feel kind of sorry for a guy who takes tuna-fish displays so seriously."

"Feeling sorry for somebody doesn't make me like him." She rubbed his wet head with her hat. But gently.

They walked along the shoulder of the highway, past gas stations and discount shoe stores and the Art Shoppe, where a woman was carrying paintings of clowns and half-nudes on black velvet back outside after the rain. They were walking in the wrong direction for Crow's house, and Polly guessed he must be walking her home. A ray of sun broke through for a moment, disappeared again.

As soon as they turned off the highway it was quieter. In the sudden stillness they were conscious of the sound of their footsteps, of the bird crying *Phoebe, Phoebe!* like a mother calling her lost child. Suddenly they felt alone.

"I'd like to show you something," Polly said. "If you have time."

"Oh, I have time."

They walked through Naomi's neighborhood. Outside her house her little brother Stewart was sailing wadded-up paper in the water flowing along the curb. On the edge of Laughing Brooks, there was an old stucco house with a crumbling roof and rusty-looking vines climbing up its walls. Surrounded by trim, prim Laughing Brooks houses, its front yard was a jungle of unpruned hedges and stunted, twisted sassafras trees. There was a big boat sinking in the side yard, its hull disintegrating into the soil. When Polly was smaller she was the only one in the neighborhood brave enough to ring the house's doorbell on Halloween.

"An old woman with her head tied up in a rag gave me two pennies. She looked more lonely than anything else. People said her husband was a fisherman years and years ago, and that she'd buried him in the back yard. Then she died, and the house has been falling down ever since."

But it wasn't the house she wanted to show him. It was the beech tree. It stood on one edge of the spook-house lawn, its trunk so thick she couldn't reach her arms around it. Its branches grew all the way down to the ground and then curved back up again, tips pointed to the sky.

"It must be really old. And look. Look what you can do."

Ducking through the tree's down-swept branches, Polly stood between them and the smooth gray trunk. "My hide-out."

Crow came in and stood beside her. The sun slipped from behind the clouds as they stood there; it shone through the bare branches and penned a little maze of shadows at their feet.

"I've loved coming in here for years now." She laid a hand on the tree's silver bark. "Especially in summer, when the leaves are full — then you can barely see out."

Crow ran his hand down the trunk, let it rest inches from hers. "It's like a small house," he said. "A small, cozy house."

"How'd you know? That's just what I've always made believe."

His hand slipped, and touched hers. And that was when they kissed for the first time.

Chapter Thirteen

"Kiss kiss! Kiss kiss!"

Naomi and Polly whirled around, and there in the living-room doorway was Stewart, dressed in pajamas, a scruffy teddy bear under his arm. Eavesdropping. "Kiss kiss!" He made a mouth like a fish.

"You're supposed to be asleep!" Naomi jumped up from the couch. She was babysitting, and Polly had just dropped by to tell her, "Yes, this afternoon, under the spook-house tree. Afterwards I'd swear he was trembling, Nome, as if he'd never kissed anyone before . . ."

"Kiss kiss!"

Naomi's other brother, Gerald, stumbled out from the bedroom and squinted in the bright light.

"Gerald kisses girls!" hooted Stewart. "Gerald loves girls! Only he's so ugly they all hate him!"

"Do you want both your knees broken with a baseball bat?" Gerald asked calmly.

"You can't catch me!" Stewart took off out of the room. "You can't catch me!"

"Excuse me, Polly."

When Naomi caught up to him Stewart was bouncing on Gerald's bed. She shooed him across the room to his own bed, while Gerald, with great dignity, not even deigning to look at them, climbed under the covers, turned his face to the wall, and fell back asleep at once. He breathed through his nose, every now and again giving a little snort, making Naomi think of her father when he fell asleep on the floor in front of the TV. Mr. and Mrs. Denning were at a PTO dance.

"Great, I'll be over around nine," Danny had said. "There's a good movie on tonight." "My parents wouldn't like it, Danny." "They don't have to know." "Well, but, what if one of my brothers wakes up?" "Yeah, okay. I'll call you, then — if I can."

Doomed to a whole night of waiting for the phone to ring. Trying to send thought messages over the wires to his house: Call me! Hey, you, call me!

"I'm scared," said Stewart, his voice small. "There's ghosts outside."

Outside the wind howled and moaned. Through the windows the bare branches, silhouetted in the street light, looked like the gnarled fingers of old men wringing their hands. Stewart was only six years old.

"It's okay, Stewie." She sat on the edge of his bed. "It's just Spring and Winter fighting it out, like Batman and the Penguin. Winter is losing, he's getting chased away, and he doesn't like it. Hear him complaining?"

Stewart lay, covers up to his chin, teddy bear wedged in beside him, listening. From the living room came the click of knitting needles and the quiet murmur of the TV. Naomi remembered how reassuring it had been, when she was small, to hear that murmur, mingled with her parents' voices, as she lay in bed at night. Once or twice she'd lain awake until her parents went to bed, and the silence and darkness of the house had terrified her. Back then she'd liked to think her parents stayed up all night long, keeping watch.

The wind shrieked; Stewart's eyes, just about to close, jerked open again. Naomi smoothed his hair, spoke to him softly.

"It's okay, it's all right." She used the same words her mother had once used to her. "I'm here." Now she was the guardian.

"Tell me a story."

"Once there was a boy named Stewart. He loved stew. Beef stew, chicken stew, old shoe stew . . ."

A new sound, a gentle *thump thump thump,* a steady bass beneath the wild brass of the wind — it was Peter, the upstairs tenant, swinging in his wicker swing chair, pushing off from the floor with one foot. He liked to sit in the chair while he watched TV or studied; sometimes Naomi heard the *thump thump thump* late into the night. When he was reading something especially interesting he thumped harder and faster. "Tch tch," Mrs. Denning would say, frowning up at the ceiling. "It's only his swing chair," Naomi would tell her, "it's not what you think." "Never you mind what I think," said Mrs. Denning.

". . . pork stew with dumplings, cauliflower stew and strawberry stew and orange Creamsicle stew . . ."

The phone rang and Naomi jumped, bouncing Stewart awake again. But Polly raced to get it, and when a moment passed and she didn't call out, Naomi knew it wasn't Danny.

"He loved stew so much his mother said, 'You will turn into stew!' and one day he did. One day when he woke up he was turned into a big pot of Hungarian goulash. It was very embarrassing . . ."

Stewart's brown eyes closed but Naomi went on sitting beside him. She wasn't eager to hear Polly crow over Crow. It was hard, when you were unhappy yourself, to share someone else's happiness, even your best friend's. Why didn't Danny call? Because of last night, at the Hideaway? Because of tonight, not letting him come over? For no reason except to make her miserable?

Naomi lightly smoothed Stewart's hair. He was asleep, trusting her, the Big Strong Sister. But Naomi didn't feel very strong. And now Crow had kissed Polly. It was hard to imagine, he was so shy, such a loner — how did he ever manage it? Probably she kissed him.

Naomi remembered back in seventh grade, when she and Crow were both in Mrs. Quinn's class. She had gone to the "Spring Fling" in the junior high cafeteria, and Crow had asked her to dance. Actually what he did wasn't so much to ask her as to come and stand silently in front of her, till at last she reached out and took his hand. It was as cold and clammy as hers was hot and dry. Crow had smelled of sweat and Ivory soap. They had danced, the last dance, a slow one, without saying a word, the two of them stiff as frozen laundry. Afterward he had mumbled, "Thank you very much," and walked away.

Thump thump thump — a heartbeat, the pounding of a swollen heart. For two whole weeks after that dance, Naomi remembered, she had hoped Crow liked her. Not that she liked him, especially. But she'd been so hungry for some boy to like her, some boy, any boy. But Crow had never said a word to her since, not in four years. And now Polly? It was hard to imagine an odder couple.

Thump-thump, thump-thump, Dan-ny, Dan-ny . . .

Stewart mumbled in his sleep, turned his head to one side, resting his cheek on the teddy bear beside him. He took little short breaths, as if he were still testing out this business of being alive, while from across the room twelve-year-old Gerald's breaths were deep and strong. Naomi pulled the covers up around Stewart, and kissed his forehead, then went and tucked Gerald in, too. In spite of everything, the peaceful kind of happiness began to creep over her, standing there beside his bed. The quiet warm house, secure against the storm outside, her two younger brothers asleep, trusting her to care for them — Naomi sighed. She could never feel this kind of peacefulness when she was with someone else. Not with Polly, her best friend, and definitely not with Danny. When I'm with Danny, she thought, it's as if I have a little alarm inside me, programmed to go off as soon as it detects his anger, or his boredom, or his looking at another girl. When I'm with him I'm always listening for the alarm to go off. Even with Polly, there's the bittersweet. Certain things I don't say, questions I can't ask. *Ding ding ding,* the alarm goes off.

I'm only myself when I'm by myself, Naomi thought, standing there in the dark bedroom. As if I'm two people. It's so much easier to be alone. But then, would I ever want to give up the me that kisses Danny? Or the me that does Instant Replay with Polly? No, no way.

It's too complicated, she decided. The boys' clock read ten thirty. Getting late for Danny to call. Naomi sighed again, and tiptoed out of the room.

Polly sat on the couch, working on the scarf Naomi was supposedly knitting Danny. She held it up, her face screwed up as if it were a dead fish.

"What are you doing to this scarf, Nome? I have never before seen a scarf shaped like a trapezoid."

Naomi sat beside her, and the sight of the scarf made her laugh. It really was the most awful scarf she had ever seen.

"I can't knit. I've decided it's one of those God-given talents, like playing the violin or writing novels or being able to lose ten pounds. Some of us have it, some of us —"

"You're dropping stitches, that's your problem. Now watch, I'll show you. See right here . . ."

Naomi watched, nodding, knowing that as soon as she was by herself she would start dropping stitches again. "Okay, I'll try," she promised, though at this rate it'd be July before she was done, and by then Danny would probably have broken up with her anyway.

Polly stood up, yawning, and dumped the knitting into Naomi's lap. "You don't like knitting, that's the real problem. One of these days you'll find something you really love to do, and then the world better watch out."

"Polly-anna."

"It's the truth! I've gotta go, I'm falling asleep watching this stupid TV movie. Oh, that was Peter who called. He said to tell you to watch the educational channel at eleven — there's something about fish reproduction on? He said he had a feeling you'd enjoy it. He has a voice like a wood flute."

"He does? Hey, you can't go! You didn't finish telling me about Crow!"

Polly flung her poncho over her head, her long red hair going all static-y where it had come loose from its braids. She gave another yawn. "I already told you. Whew, I'm dead — that Atwater's a sadist. Oh, and Peter said something about a pit? You two sure have a weird friendship, pits and fish . . ."

She moved toward the front door. Though a moment before Naomi had been dreading hearing Polly talk about Crow, now she was all curiosity.

"You can't do this to me! Tell me half a story and leave me hanging — you're worse than a two-part movie!"

"I told you, I told you. By the way, I hope Danny calls you, the creep."

"Don't change the subject."

"You want all the gory details? How his glasses steamed up? They did — he forgot to take them off."

"Just tell me one thing. Do you think — do you really think —"

"I was the first girl he ever kissed?" Polly guessed Naomi's thought, as usual. She was the one person who knew Naomi's secret: Danny was the first and only boy who had ever kissed her.

"Yeah. Do you think?"

Polly pulled open the front door, letting in a gust of air that flapped the doily on the hall table. She ran down the front steps, her poncho flying out in the wind. "I'll tell you a secret," she called up from the foot of the steps. "It seemed — it seemed like the first time for me, too!"

And then she was gone, like one of the papery leaves flung about in the wind, and Naomi was left wondering, Was that just the glow from the porch light? Or could she possibly have seen Polly blush?

Chapter Fourteen

Life was unfair. Naomi slumped back down on the couch and stared gloomily at the TV. Real life, that is. In TV life, look — all that girl had to do was wash her hair with Fresh 'n' Free, and a whole beachful of men fell to their knees. Or that woman — she rubbed on a little herbal skin cream — bang! Prince Charming was leaning across a candle-lit table, pouring her wine. Maybe, thought Naomi, what I need is some of that perfume, the one that "will, simply, change your life."

Polly's life was like a TV commercial. One long fairy tale. Naomi sighed. The TV movie came back on. It was more than half over, but Naomi knew it would take only two minutes to figure out what was happening. She turned the volume down so she'd be sure to hear the phone when it rang. If it rang.

The movie was an old one, nothing but one car chase after another. Cars cars cars — yuck. The shipwrecked red convertible, Donny's car — the horse used to be the big macho symbol, Polly said, but it's been replaced by the car.

Naomi got up and went into the kitchen, made herself a frozen waffle, spread it with strawberry jam, and ate it with her fingers. "One serving: 410 calories," she read on the box. "Average serving size: 2." Well, might as well have an average serving. She swallowed the second one quickly, so the calories wouldn't have a chance to stick. *Thump thump thump* went the swing upstairs. The kitchen clock said eleven. Wondering what made Peter think she'd be interested in the sex life of fish, she went back into the living room and idly flipped from a car careening through a roadblock to the educational channel.

At first she wasn't sure what she was looking at. It appeared to be a sunset come to life.

"The brittle sea larva," the narrator told her, "is but one of the sea's jewellike children."

Without taking her eyes from the set, Naomi backed over to the couch and sat down, wadding up Danny's scarf in her lap. One after another the little hatchlings appeared on the screen. Crab, sea urchin, starfish larvae — translucent, brightly colored, they were like liquid crystals, melting rubies and sapphires. Naomi watched as a jellyfish was born. "Budding, asexual reproduction," the man's voice intoned, as the little rainbowed creature detached itself from what looked like a pile of saucers, and floated away.

Asexual? What was that? And what were those creatures —

plants or animals? Look at the colors — strings of jewels, neon lights, so eerily, strangely beautiful that Naomi shuddered. Their movements and their shapes were as liquid as the sea, so gracefully fluid it seemed any moment they might dissolve and reform as something else. Now, here, here at last was something she recognized: a whale. A mother whale, giving birth. A baby whale, weighing one ton, was born there in the Denning living room. Naomi watched the father watch: he was smiling, a wide crooked smile. And then, he sang, a wild, mournful-joyful sound, somewhere between a wolf and an electronic synthesizer. The song bounced back from the sea bottom, an echo in harmony with itself.

Then slowly another sound began to break in on her — strange, jangling, discordant . . .

The phone was ringing.

"Naomi? Are you okay?"

"Huh? Oh, Danny. Hi. Yeah, I'm okay." She'd dragged his scarf along with her when she jumped up, and a thin blue trail straggled across the kitchen linoleum and around the corner into the living room.

"Were you in bed already?"

If she pulled the cord as far as it could go, and held the receiver a little way from her ear, she could just get a glimpse of the TV. "No, I wasn't in bed."

"What?"

"No," she repeated, this time into the phone. Two octopuses were mating; it had to be seen to be believed.

"Well, what took you so long to answer, then? I let the phone ring at least ten times."

"You did?" The mother octopus laid two hundred thousand eggs in the walls of a sea cave, and prepared to fight off all predators.

"Well, four times anyway." His voice rose. "I was getting worried about you. What were you doing?"

It occurred to Naomi she could ask him what *he'd* been doing, that made him wait till so late to call her. But then she would have to listen to his answer, and all she wanted was to get back to the TV. "I was taking a bath."

"Oh."

"And as a matter of fact I'm standing here in a towel freezing to death so goodbye."

Naomi raced back into the living room, scrambling up the blue yarn into a hopeless tangle. Sea slugs! What an ugly name for such beautiful creatures. They were dancing together, indigo and gold, dappled and striped. Then Naomi saw a coral reef, looking just like a castle, with fish of every color darting in and out.

"Fish are color blind," said the TV voice, "so why this wealth of color? What purpose does this extravagant beauty serve?"

Upstairs the thumping went on. Outside Winter and Spring waged battle. But Naomi sat oblivious, feeling as if she were floating, and the skeins of blue yarn on the couch beside her were nothing more than small pools of sky and sea.

Chapter Fifteen

"It was just incredible. Too bad Polly left and missed it. I have to tell her about it. You should've seen those octopuses mating — ooh, it was creepy and exciting at the same time. All that beautiful rubbery skin oozing and . . . what's that word? Oscillating? Undulating?"

From behind his Sunday paper, Mr. Denning gave a cough. His wife, washing the chicken they'd eat for dinner, didn't seem to hear. Naomi reached for another doughnut.

"But the poor mother octopus! She lays all those eggs, two hundred thousand of them, and then she starves to death. She never leaves the sea cave, in case something might get in and eat her eggs. So finally they hatch, and swim out of the cave — and *then* they get eaten. Guess how many survive, out of two hundred thousand? One or two. And listen to *this:* there's a fish that can actually change its *sex* . . ."

Stewart came running into the kitchen stark naked.

"Gerald's calling me names! He said —"

Gerald strode in in pants and no shirt. "All I said —"

"He called my dingy a name!"

Naomi stuffed a piece of doughnut into her mouth. Her father rattled the Sports section.

"I thought I told you two to change out of those church clothes!" Mrs. Denning would have personally escorted Stewart to his room if her hands hadn't been covered with chicken fat. She stood holding them up by her face and exclaimed, "You march right back and put something on, Stewart Joseph Denning, and then we'll talk about . . . about names."

"But he called my —"

"All I said was, 'It's not a dingy it's a penis' and it is, so there." Gerald, who had just had sex education in school, regarded his little brother condescendingly. Naomi choked on her doughnut. Stewart began to cry. "That's right, isn't it, Ma?" asked Gerald. "That's what it's called."

Mrs. Denning went to the sink and began scrubbing her hands. "That's right," she said, rubbing away. "Now you two go get dressed before you catch your death of cold, and then you can each have one of those nice jelly doughnuts Daddy bought, how about that?" She shoved Stewart toward the door.

"Anyway," he said to Gerald. "You said it was called peanuts."

"Peanuts!" roared Gerald, forgetting his dignity. "Oh boy, are you dumb! A regular retard!"

"Sale on hamburg down at Wally's, Margaret," came from behind Mr. Denning's paper.

His wife, a soft, round woman who still wore her hair long because he wanted her to, stared at the ceiling. "I really must speak to Gerald's teachers, and find out exactly—"

"It's only the truth, Ma," Naomi said impatiently. "It's just the facts of life, that's all. You know—fish do it, people do it. Polly's mother told her about it when she was lots younger than Gerald." And Polly told me, only I thought she was making it up. I wouldn't speak to her for a week.

"Catherine Quinn is a very strong woman who is doing a brave and difficult thing, raising two children alone. But if you ask me she's almost too independent for her own good. There's something hard as nails about that woman. She should have remarried."

"Gossip doesn't become you, Margaret," issued from the Living section.

"At least she's not afraid to speak the truth," said Naomi, getting up and rinsing her dishes. "The plain *naked* truth," she added, but her mother ignored that one and went on stuffing the chicken. Roast chicken, mashed potatoes, peas, pie and ice cream: Sunday dinner every single Sunday as far back as Naomi's memory reached. The eleventh commandment must be: Thou shalt eat roast chicken on the Sabbath.

When her mother had the chicken in the oven she sat down with the books from the dry-cleaning business. Mrs.

Denning loved bookkeeping; it was what she'd done before she was married. Keeping the books accurate down to the penny was her pride and pleasure. Numbers are so tidy, she liked to say, no loose ends or jagged edges. You can't argue with a column of figures, she would say happily.

Mr. Denning folded up his paper, went into the living room, and turned on a bowling tournament. After dinner he'd turn on a golf match, and fall asleep. It was his one day off. Sunday afternoons. Naomi had always hated them. What was Polly doing now? Planting seeds with Crow? Riding around with Boom Boom? And Danny? She didn't even want to think about Danny, where he was till after eleven last night, how he'd react to her hanging up on him. Being used, it's the worst, Polly said. As if she knew. Being used was probably better than being dumped. Less lonely, anyway.

Naomi wandered from kitchen to living room to bedroom and back again, as restless, her mother said, as a thief in church. At last she said she was going upstairs to thank Peter for telling her about the program last night. She pretended not to hear her mother cluck her tongue.

Tess answered the door, dressed in a faded plaid bathrobe so big it had to be Peter's. Her curly hair hadn't been combed yet, and her eyes were a little swollen, as if she'd just waked up. Or been crying.

"Oh hi. Come on in."

"You just got up. I'll come back."

"Come in. We could use some company."

The apartment had three rooms: a bedroom, a combination kitchen–living room, and the room Tess used for a studio. There was hardly any furniture, but more books than Naomi had ever seen outside a library. Most of them seemed to have titles that ended in "ology," but there were big heavy books of drawings and paintings, too. They were piled in cardboard boxes and wooden packing crates and jammed into the one genuine bookcase; they held down the corners of the big square of fabric Tess was getting ready to linoleum print. Tess's batiks, watercolors, and pastels were pinned to the walls, and in the center of the room was her enormous scrap-metal sculpture, *Construction #1*. The day Tess brought it home from school it had taken all three of them, sweating and grunting, to get it up the stairs. Naomi had been glad her parents weren't home to see that; she could imagine what they'd say. Today *Construction #1* had a shoe of Peter's lodged in one angle, as if someone had thrown it there.

Peter was in the corner, in the "kitchen," stirring something on the stove. The stereo played Judy Collins.

"I wanted to thank you for calling me last night."

"Great, great! Just a minute, this is almost ready. Want some spaghetti?"

"No thanks. I just had breakfast."

"How about some tea?" offered Tess.

"Okay."

Tess poured her a cup from the pot on the table. The pot and mugs were beautiful, heavy and rounded, and glazed with a sea-blue design. Tess or one of her friends must have made them.

"Honey?"

"No thanks." Calories. Naomi always felt fat around Tess. Tess herself took a big spoonful, slowly and thoughtfully stirred it into her tea.

From the corner Peter yelled, "The colander! Tess, where's the damn colander?"

"Right on the damn table, full of damn bills," she answered, making no move to hand it to him.

Peter, holding the steaming spaghetti pot in one hand, reached over, grabbed the colander, and dumped it upside down, sending slips of paper fluttering all over the floor. He danced back to the sink, flourishing his colander like a conductor with his baton, and poured out the spaghetti. A plate whirled out of the cupboard, a fork twinkled between his fingers, and, *"Voilà!* Your breakfast is served, Mademoiselle Malone. *Specialité de la maison,* spaghetti à la Jacobi!" He bowed from the waist, holding it out to Tess. Naomi turned to laugh with her.

"I lost my appetite," she said, standing up abruptly and going into the bedroom. The door shut and Judy Collins stopped singing at the same moment. The stereo clicked off. Dead silence.

Peter froze, bent over, steaming spaghetti still extended. Naomi studied the little blob of doughnut jelly on the tip of her shoe. Then her wart. Finally Peter straightened up. "These temperamental artists," he said. "Come and have some spaghetti with me, Naomi Macaroni."

Naomi sat down, the flutter of bills at her feet. Peter put two plates of spaghetti on the table. The spaghetti was green. He saw Naomi's face and laughed.

"It's artichoke spaghetti. It's very nutritious, according to Tess. Put a lot of margarine on it." He took a big slab and spread it on his.

Naomi was about to tell him she was on a diet, for real this time, when the bedroom door opened and Tess came out, dressed in jeans and sweater and red-and-black-plaid lumberjack jacket. She sat in the swing and began to pull on high boots.

"Going out?" Peter tried to sound casual. Naomi nervously took a bite of the green spaghetti. She hadn't expected to witness a fight, even this non-yelling variety. "Going somewhere?"

"You're so perceptive, Peter." Tess's head was bent over her boots.

"Can I ask you where?"

"I just have to get out."

"If you can wait ten minutes I'll come with you."

"That's all right." She stood up, went to the door. "I'll be back. Probably." The door closed behind her. A second later it opened again. "Goodbye, Naomi."

"Bye," said Naomi, too loudly, her mouth full of spaghetti.

Peter stared at the door a moment, as if hoping it would open for a third time and Tess would say, "I'm sorry. I'll wait for you." But the door stayed closed. Naomi knew just how Peter felt. A door that stayed closed was as bad as a phone that didn't ring. In sympathy she took another big bite of spaghetti. It tasted like shredded turnips.

"Delicious," she said.

"It's awful, isn't it? Tess is a health-food fanatic. Between you and me, my favorite food is Hostess Twinkies. Don't tell Tess, though, or she'll walk out on me."

The joke fell somewhat flat, considering. Peter wasn't really the joking type, after all, and the effort seemed to have worn him out. Gloomily, he attacked the green spaghetti. Though she wasn't sure he wanted to talk at all, Naomi decided to tell him how much she'd enjoyed the TV show last night. His face lit up; he slapped his open palm on the rickety table, tipping over the dish of all-natural sea salt.

"Wasn't that fantastic? Of course it was all put in popular language, grossly oversimplified, even romanticized — but wasn't the photography something else? What'd you think of the grouper?"

"Is that the one that changes from a female to a male?"

"Right. It can also change its coloring, from yellow to red or solid to spotted, within seconds. A real schizophrenic, the grouper."

"Peter, how does it do that?"

"Change its sex, you mean? Hermaphroditism is fairly common among sea creatures." He began to talk about ovaries and testes, sperm and eggs, as offhandedly as if he were describing how to make a peanut butter sandwich. He soon lost her, using words like "mitosis" and "meiosis," "gametes" and "deoxyribonucleic acid." Some of it had a faintly familiar ring, from last year's course in biology, but most of it was just something she'd learned for a test and forgotten the next day. She wasn't sure which was worse, her parents' palpitations over the word *penis* or this mechanical list of facts.

"But I mean — *how* do they do it?" she asked when she could get a word in.

Peter looked confused. He took Naomi's cold spaghetti and began to eat it. "I just told you how."

"But I mean . . ." Naomi tried to recapture the sense of amazement she had felt last night. "I mean, doesn't it just knock you over, the *strange*ness of it?"

" 'There are more things in heaven and earth, Horatio, than are dreamt of in your philosophy.' That's from *Hamlet*. Have you ever read *Hamlet?*"

"No."

"Well, you should. The sea, Naomi Macaroni, is the source of life. Your great-great-great-great-et-cetera-grandmother crawled up out of the sea, you know. The first fish that had the nerve to do that — wow. It must have had lungs, that was essential, and its fins must have evolved to a limblike state." He tipped his chair back on two legs and stared at the ceiling, then suddenly brought it back down with a small crash. "I bet you didn't know that whales were once land creatures, did you? That's right. Whales were once strolling around on land, going about their business just like baboons and alley cats and cockroaches, but for some reason they couldn't make it on land and so went back to the sea. There is a stage in the gestation of every whale when it has legs. Hind legs. Of course they almost never develop; they disappear. But whales with legs have been found, now imagine that."

"Are you making that up?"

"When it comes to biology, truth is often stranger than fiction. Especially marine biology. Only it's not strange at all, really — survival is what it comes down to. Each species deals with the problems of food and reproduction in the most efficient way possible." He tilted his chair back again and peered up at a cobweb. "Of course Tess hates to hear me talk this way. 'Why do you always have to understand everything?' she says to me. 'Can't you just say it's wonderful, and be amazed, and leave it at that?' I tell her understanding only makes it all the more wonderful. But she gets with her artsy friends, who think all scientists have computers instead of hearts, and . . . When I come home from lab, from dissecting something, she won't even come near me." He thumped his chair back down and stared at Naomi.

"It's hard to share enthusiasms," she heard herself say. "It's like trying to tell someone your dream. Something gets lost."

He looked at her. "You're right. Only it's impossible *not* to try and share them, with someone you care about."

"I know."

"A dilemma."

"Yes."

"I thought you'd like that program last night. Polly said, 'What? Fish reproduction?' But I said, 'Tell Naomi. I have a feeling she'll like it.'"

"Why'd you think that?"

He shrugged, picking up the dishes and dumping them in the sink. "I can tell you have an instinct for beauty."

The blush. Naomi picked at her wart.

"What are you thinking of doing after high school?"

"I might be a secretary, or a bookkeeper." *Might?*

"No way," said Peter, lighting his pipe. "No offense to secretaries, but uh-uh. No, you should be, let me see . . ." He sat back, pulled on his pipe. "You should run your own greenhouse. Or work in a nature preserve. Or how about a famous nature photographer?"

"Oh yeah, sure. And whales can walk."

"Does an ant believe in central air conditioning?"

"Huh?"

"Just because a thing's outside your experience doesn't mean it's impossible."

He walked Naomi to the door. She saw the hopeful look on his face as he opened it, as if maybe Tess would still be standing out there, playing a trick on him. Naomi had to resist the impulse to reach out and touch his furry head.

"Bye, Peter."

"You should come up more often."

"Thanks."

At the downstairs door Naomi smelled the chicken roasting, heard a muffled cheer go up from the bowling tournament, thought of the book report due tomorrow. Instead of going in she soundlessly reached inside the door, grabbed the old sweatshirt hanging on a peg, and slipped it on. She wheeled her bike out of the garage and pedaled out to the woods.

This time she walked all the way around them, the way she'd meant to with Danny. So quiet. Only the slow, sad call of the mourning dove and the rustle, now and then, of some small startled creature in the undergrowth. It was cold, but she didn't mind. When she came to the shipwrecked car she looked inside and saw what she hadn't had a chance to notice last time: fiddleheads, young ferns, curled up like babies' fists, were sprouting on the rotting floor. The skunk cabbage stretched brilliant green leaves to the sun. She crouched beside them, on the edge of the mud.

You have an instinct for beauty, he said.

The rusty leaves of last year's hepaticas were still there. Brushing them aside, Naomi found the buds of this spring's flowers. Small bowed heads, covered with down. Hatchlings of the sea, hatchlings of the forest. She touched the buds with one finger, smiling, wondering if that was how Peter's head would feel.

She must have stayed in the woods longer than she thought. By the time she got home she was cold, and there was a streak of sunset showing near the horizon. She wheeled her bike into the garage, her hands blue, knowing her mother would have a fit at how late she was. Still, she lingered outside a moment longer, reluctant to have the spell of the afternoon broken. There was a little patch of ice on the driveway, and as Naomi stood there it began to take on the color of the sunset, to turn pale coral.

The sky at my feet.

"Naomi Marie Denning, where have you been? I've been worried sick. Your dinner's stone cold. I called up to Peter hours ago and he said —"

"I know, Ma. I'm sorry. Just a minute." Naomi hurried to the phone and dialed Danny's number. Look out and see the sunset, she'd say.

But his mother told her Danny'd been out all day, and wasn't home yet.

Chapter Sixteen

"... symbiosis. There's a little gray-and-blue fish, I forget its name, that lives side by side with the giant Portuguese man-of-war jellyfish. The real nasty kind of jellyfish, you know, with long tentacles hanging down from it like gargantuan spaghetti. It stings its prey to death, and then eats it. But . . ." Naomi was almost out of breath, trying to talk and keep up with Danny, who seemed to be out to set a new record for getting from one end of the school to the other. "But this tiny blue-and-gray fish I'm telling you about swims right along with it, in and out of the tentacles, and is never harmed. Isn't that amazing?"

"Super fish," said Danny, charging around a corner.

"No, it's just a regular little fish, but the two of them have adapted to each other. The fish acts as decoy. It attracts other fish for the man-of-war to eat, and at the same time it's protected because nothing ever dares attack those giant stinging jellyfish. Believe me, it's a cold, cruel world down in that ocean. I wish I could remember that little fish's name." Actually Naomi remembered its name quite well — nomeus — but she didn't want Danny to think she was showing off. "Symbiosis, living together for mutual benefit. It's something they all have to learn, down there in the depths."

"Why are you suddenly so interested in jellyfish? I didn't think that Peter guy was so good-looking."

"What are you talking about? Here I am trying to tell you something interesting, and that's all you can think of to say?"

"Marsh!" Danny reached out and punched Marcia Melon, who smiled sweetly and continued on down the hall, leaving behind her usual smog of Ambush perfume. Naomi was beginning to get a stitch in her side.

"Danny, are you in training for a marathon or something?"

He didn't answer. It was as if he were doing her a big favor, walking her to lunch. He'd been acting this way all week, and though it was Friday he still hadn't mentioned anything about the weekend. Once or twice it had been on the tip of Naomi's tongue to say, "What's going on? Can't we talk about this?" But somehow she kept swallowing the words, half in anger, half in fear of what he'd say. Maybe if she made believe nothing was wrong, things would just slip back to the way they were before.

"Here's another example. There's a striped fish called the clown fish, and —"

"Have you come across the cold fish yet?"

The bell rang, like the signal for the end of a boxing round. Naomi stood, gaping, at the cafeteria door, as he disappeared around the corner.

"No, but I've read about dinosaurs with brains the size of walnuts," she said to the empty air.

"Nome, do you feel okay?" Polly took her elbow.

In the cafeteria Naomi tried to write him a note. Polly looked at Naomi's tray, the congealing chicken à la king and melting ice-cream sandwich, and said, "If I were you I'd ignore him."

"I guess I'm not you."

"Nome, let's go to the thrift shop after school. They're having their annual spring-cleaning sale."

"What? You're not going to Crow's?" Polly had been going there every afternoon that week, which hadn't helped ease Naomi's feeling of abandonment.

"He has to work at Wally's."

"Oh, I see."

"Maybe afterwards I could teach you to make bread. It's almost Easter, time for kulich."

"Look, you don't have to feel sorry for me." Naomi crumpled up the note.

"He's playing games with your head, Nome." Polly reached over and tapped Naomi's temple. "He's just like a little boy — he can't have his way, so he sulks. Boys are always less mature than girls, you know. What was my mother saying? Their developmental age is usually a year or more behind their chronological age, and the fact is — this is a fact now — they never do catch up. Males are always one step behind females." She watched Naomi push a hunk of coagulated chicken through a pile of cold rice. "Nome?"

"I don't see you minding Crow's development."

"Uh-oh. I fear I detect symptoms of the Cinderella Effect."

"The what?"

"Cinderella Effect. You know, women getting into a fight over a man."

"I guess you're Cinderella, and I'm the jealous stepsister?"

"This girl wallows in self-pity, absolutely wallows."

"Okay, okay, you're right. I'll go to the thrift shop with you."

After last period Polly headed down the hall to Naomi's locker — and did an abrupt about-face. Danny was standing there. He was quietly kicking the locker door while Naomi stared at the floor and talked. Polly circled around the school once; when she came back he was still there and Naomi was still talking. Her expression was as earnest as if she were in court, and Danny was shaking his head. Polly circled the school again, and when she came back this time Naomi was alone, hurling gym shoes and textbooks around inside the locker and mumbling to herself.

"Nome?"

She jumped, looked up. "Oh, it's you. Let's get out of here." She slammed the locker so hard it twanged.

Polly waited for her to say what had happened, but Naomi marched along without saying a word. That is, at first she marched. By the end of the school driveway the marching had become walking, then trudging, and by the time they arrived at the Methodist Church Trash 'n' Treasures, Naomi was barely dragging herself along. Still she hadn't said a word. As they went down the steps to the church basement, past banners that said JOY, LOVE, and PEACE, Polly broke the silence at last.

"Have you learned any more fish facts from Peter lately?"

Naomi lifted her head. "Last night he told me more about the grouper. Can you imagine it — being both sexes in one lifetime? I think it's better than reincarnation. It's creepy, I know, but still there's something about it being able to *transform* itself that way that really gets to me. And the groupers aren't the only ones who do it, either. Peter knows everything about the sexual — oh, hello, Mrs. Gripp."

"Good afternoon!" Hands on hips, the dumpling-cheeked lady who ran the shop stood glaring up at them. She pulled her white cardigan closer about her, as if protecting herself from these girls who talked so glibly about groupers (that had something to do with rock stars, didn't it?) and lessons from Peter in sexual who knew what. She gave a righteous sniff. "Everything is half price, including the Bibles," she informed them, and stalked stiffly back to her desk.

Polly began trying on hats, her shoulders shaking with held-in laughter. Blushing furiously, Naomi whispered, "Anyway, as soon as it gets warmer, Peter's taking me to the real ocean to show me the tide pools. He says it's no good trying to observe marine life around here — the beaches are too polluted."

Polly pulled a brown felt hat from a bin and tried it on. "You talk about Peter an awful lot lately," she teased. "You never say a word about Tess."

"I think they're having problems. She wasn't home last night when I went up there. Peter said she was at school working on a project, but I could tell he was listening for her steps on the stairs the whole time."

"Maybe he was afraid she'd be jealous, catching you two alone together." Polly pulled the brim of the hat down, spylike.

"That'll be the day. He's so in love with Tess it hurts to look at him." Naomi heaved a huge sigh. "He cares more about Tess than about biology, even. But I don't think she came home last night. I listened and I never heard her come in. Peter sat up thumping half the night. My mother was wild."

Polly laughed, taking off the hat and twirling it on a finger. She was wearing a dress that would have looked like a tablecloth on anyone else, and her hair was swept back in little-girl plastic barrettes, two yellow birds. "What do you think of this hat?"

"Anything looks good on you, Pol."

"Not for me, for Crow. I want to give him a present. He gave me one yesterday, and I want us to be even."

Naomi swallowed a sigh. "What'd he give you?"

"An African violet."

"Oh no — you're going to try and keep an African violet? They're hard — you have to feed them, and really care for them."

Polly laughed again. "Don't worry. Guess what? I think your beggaronia's coming back to life." She held up her thumb and peered at it. "I see a tinge of green."

"You really like Crow, don't you?"

"What's that got to do with anything? Ooh, look at this one — this'd be perfect for Danny." Polly reached in the hat bin and fished out a cowboy hat. "When he's doing his Clint Eastwood, Macho Man act."

"I would appreciate your not mocking Danny."

"I'm sorry."

Naomi blinked. Had she ever heard Polly utter those two words before?

"I'm sorry," Polly said again. "I'm just afraid he'll hurt you . . . What I really meant to say was, I'm glad you're getting into biology like this, Nome. You need to find something you can throw yourself into."

"Yeah, like a ditch." Turning her back, Naomi fingered an old flannel shirt.

"You had a fight."

"I should've known you'd know."

"Tell me."

"He asked me to go out with him tomorrow. Donny and the Doorknob are driving out to Pumpkin Notch." Pumpkin Notch was a state park on the ocean. " 'We could go for a nice long walk,' he said, 'and talk.' So I said, 'I've been trying to talk to you all week. I didn't know we had to drive all the way out to Pumpkin Notch to have a conversation.' "

"Good for you."

"Then he tried to make as if he'd arranged the whole trip just for me, since I have this new interest in the ocean. I said, 'Danny, you never used to lie to me.' 'What!' he yelled. I said, 'You know you really couldn't care less about the ocean or my interest in it. You know you start to yawn the minute I open my mouth about it. Or about anything, for that matter.' "

"Whew."

"I said, 'Admit it, it's not just walking and talking you have in mind now, is it?'"

"Ahem!" Mrs. Gripp gave a sharp rap on her desk.

Naomi went on more softly. "I said, 'What are you trying to prove, Danny? You don't have to prove anything to me, you know.' He said I was destroying his ego. I said that was his problem."

"You did?"

"I don't know what came over me. Then he said I never tried to see things from his point of view, and I thought I was so much better than him, showing off with all this talk about symbiosis and such. I said he was crazy, I never thought that. He said one minute I acted like I wanted him and the next like I didn't, and the trouble with me was I didn't know *what* I wanted. So I said, 'Maybe that's true, but you aren't helping me find out.' I told him, 'You play games with my head.'"

"Well well well." Polly flung Danny's hat back into the bin.

"It felt good for about three seconds. Ever since I've been considering various methods of suicide."

"You don't need him, Nome."

"I don't?"

"You don't need someone so insecure he puts you down because you know things he doesn't."

Here came the lecture. "You always make it sound so black and white, Pol."

"Well, it is."

No, it's not. Naomi fingered the old flannel shirt. If you can say that, she thought, you've never really cared for a boy. When you do, the edges blur, your happiness and his run together.

"And the other thing. It's *your* body . . ."

Mrs. Gripp staggered up from her chair, clutching her desk with white knuckles.

". . . and your decision," Polly went on in a lower tone, and she was off on her lecture, a lecture she could give because *rejection* was a foreign word to Polly Quinn.

Only half listening, Naomi flipped through the pile of old, tossed-out shirts. Why did I say that to him, "You play games with my head?" I was only echoing Polly, who hardly even knows him. It's not that he plays games — it's that he doesn't know exactly what *he* wants, either, only what he's *supposed* to want. Naomi thought of the way he laughed, that childlike side of him that sent a softness all through her. Maybe if I hadn't been so ready to accuse him — wasn't there a moment there, when I told him he didn't have to prove anything to me — he looked at me then, and I could tell I'd said something . . . But no, I had to accuse, I had to be a parrot, a parrot for Polly, who still this very minute is telling me how I should think, what I should do.

In Naomi's mind there appeared a diagram she'd seen in one of Peter's books: a dissected dog shark, pinned to a board for inspection, each of its parts labeled and explained.

Polly bought the felt hat and they left, to Mrs. Gripp's immense relief. Outside, Polly said that Crow would be surprised, since she'd told him how much she disliked presents. "He'll never expect me to give him one."

Without letting herself think, Naomi blurted out, "You say you worry about me — did you ever stop to notice Crow's the kind who gets hurt easily, too?"

Chapter Seventeen

"Ouch!"

As they walked across the park together, Polly pinched Crow on the wrist.

"What'd I do to deserve that?"

"Just testing," Polly said, "how easily you get hurt."

It was spring now. The calendar said so. The teachers in Cass's school said so. They had taken the shamrocks and kites down from the bulletin boards and replaced them with Easter bunnies and tulips. The leaves of real tulips spiraled up in gardens everywhere.

But the season liked to tease. Yesterday, standing bare-armed and bare-toed in Crow's back yard, Polly had read the bean package: " 'Pencil Pod Wax. Plant when all danger of frost is past.' Okay, let's go."

"Oh no," Crow had said. "The cold weather's not over yet."

"You're such a pessimist," she had told him, pushing the lock of black hair out of his eyes. "There's not going to be any more frost."

Today it was twenty-five degrees.

The only other person in the park was a woman with a terrier that yapped ferociously at Polly's secondhand fur coat. Crow wore the felt hat she'd bought him at the thrift shop, and carried a bag of stale popcorn.

"Here ducky ducky ducky," Polly called, standing on the edge of the pond. The day made her giddy. The wind whisked the thin white clouds across the sky like cloths whipped from a blue enamel table. The trees' shadows disappeared, reappeared, disappeared — a magic show. "Here, you fat old things, come and get your treat!"

The white ducks, sleek and glossy from their winter indoors, gobbled up the popcorn Polly and Crow tossed them. His father had brought it home last night, the theater's leftovers. Farther out on the water was a swan; shyer, or prouder, it didn't come near them. Crow tossed a handful out to it but the yellow shower seemed to frighten it, and it glided farther away.

After they'd thrown all the popcorn they sat together on a bench, huddled close against the cold.

"Remember back in fifth grade, when you threw up during the spring concert? Right in the middle of 'Daffy Down Dilly'?"

Crow pulled his new-old hat down over his eyes. "I still have bad dreams about that."

"Oh no!"

"Yeah, I do. Luckily I was in the front row, so I didn't get anyone. Only Mrs. Cazzaza's feet. Blah!"

Polly laughed, snuggling against him. She could barely feel him, between her fur coat and his down jacket. She touched his bare neck, to make sure he was in there. "I hated that song anyway." She began to sing, " 'Daffy Down Dilly has come to town . . .' "

" 'Dressed in her shining yellow gown . . .' "

" 'A cup of sunshine is her face . . .' "

" 'Her slender neck so full of grace . . .' I used to sing *grapes*," Crow said. "I thought her neck was supposed to be full of grapes."

"No wonder you threw up."

They watched the swan glide to where some of the popcorn still bobbed on the dark surface of the pond. All at once it darted its shining black bill and plucked up one piece, then another.

"I hate popcorn."

Polly raised her head from Crow's shoulder and looked at him in astonishment. "But I thought you said your father always brought it home for a treat."

"I'm sick of the stuff. I can't stand the sight of it. But I always eat it. I don't want to hurt his feelings."

She laid her head back on his shoulder. "You're crazy. I'd never eat anything I hated. Like peas. Yuck!"

"You just wait and see how good those peas are going to taste, Polly Quinn — you just wait! You'll gobble them down!" He tried to tickle her through the fur coat.

"Uh-uh, not me!" She wriggled away, giving him a little push that made his glasses go crooked on his nose. He glanced around to make sure no one was looking, then took the glasses off and kissed her solemnly. Once, twice. Polly took the glasses and put them on her own nose. "Why don't you just throw the popcorn away when your father's not home?"

"I don't know. It'd be too sad. He thinks it's a big treat for me."

"You're crazy," she said again. "You sound like you're the father and he's the kid."

Crow squinted out at the pond. "Yeah, well, it's just the two of us, so we have to take care of each other."

"Crow, you look like something out of *The Faceless.*" Behind his gold-rimmed glasses, Polly crossed her eyes. "How can you see through these things?"

"Give me those." He took them off her nose, kissed her quickly. She put her head back on his shoulder, and they watched the swan finish the popcorn that bloomed on the water like tiny yellow water lilies. It was only two weeks since they'd first kissed beneath the spook-house tree; yet he had told her so much about himself, it seemed much longer. He had told her: that his mother was killed in a car accident on the way home from getting her hair done, that he played the recorder and didn't know how to dance, that last summer he'd worked in a factory and Wally's was a picnic by comparison, that he was saving up to go to music school or buy a motorcycle and go cross-country (he still didn't know which), that the first day he talked to her in Wally's he kept waiting to wake up, that once in seventh grade he danced with Naomi, but he could tell she didn't like him. And now, tightening his arm around her, he told her, "Do you know you're the first girl I've ever gone out with?"

"You shouldn't tell me that."

"Why not?"

"If you don't know, I can't tell you. Remember when we used to say that all the time, back in, what was it — fourth grade? Now Cass is saying it. It's taken the place of 'retarded.' For a while there she was saying everything was retarded — teachers, friends she was mad at, Catherine — once she even said *God* was retarded because —"

"How come you're so good at changing the subject?"

"That's what Nome always says!"

"It's a bad habit."

"Would you rather have me bite my nails? Or chew tobacco?"

"Well, it is. Teasing is a bad habit."

She touched his chin. "You know, if you grew a beard I bet you'd look just like Abraham Lincoln. Honest Abe, that's what I'll call you."

He told her everything. It was as if for sixteen years one coin after another, bright and tarnished, big and small, had been saved up in a glass jar — and that jar had suddenly shattered, spilling the treasure out in every direction, showering Polly.

"Crow?" She looked up at him, under the brim of his hat.

"Well, you are, you know. You are the first girl. I didn't think you'd mind."

He thought she was laughing at him. "I don't mind."

But still the lips that surprised her with their softness stayed set in a straight line. It had something to do with his father and the popcorn; somehow that and thinking she was laughing at him were all tangled together. She reached up and traced a smile over his frown.

"I don't mind. Know what I was thinking? It's too bad this isn't a TV show. Then we could introduce your father to my mother, and of course they'd fall in love right off. After all kinds of hilarious complications they'd get married, and you and I'd be stepbrother and stepsister. Except you'd need a little brother, to balance Cass — they like things to be neat and tidy on TV. Let's see, it could be called . . . ummm . . . 'Two Plus Two'? 'The Instant Family'? He's not smiling." She tickled his chin. "He doesn't think it's funny, does he? I wonder why."

"If you don't know, I can't tell you." He kissed her again, without even checking to see if anyone watched. Then he stood up. "I almost forgot. I have something to show you."

Holding hands — he always held her hand, as if to reassure himself she was really there — they crossed the park and walked the few blocks to his house. Polly could close her eyes and see this street; it was strange, but she could never walk down it without a feeling of déjà vu. In the tiny front yard there was one bush.

"When it blooms I'll bring you lilacs every day."

They walked through the house, Polly switching off the

hall light, and into the kitchen. Spread on the table were a newspaper, a mug of cold coffee, and a box of Danish, the remains of Crow's father's breakfast-lunch. He went to work at two every day, rarely got home before midnight, and Polly still hadn't met him. Crow picked up the mug and carefully balanced it atop the mountain of dirty dishes already in the sink. He held open the back door for her.

"Surprise."

The peas were up. Together they crouched over them. Where yesterday there had been nothing but bare earth, now pale, folded green leaves — small clasped hands — reached for the sun.

"They're beautiful," she said, and felt a catch in her throat. It was as if she'd never really expected them to come up. As if she'd been given a present she didn't deserve.

Chapter Eighteen

Presents. Before she knew how it happened she and Crow were giving each other presents all the time. She gave him the hat from the thrift shop, a book on the stars — "This summer I'll teach you all the constellations" — then a loaf of her mother's health bread — sawdust bread, Cass called it — to replace the sugary junk food he and his father ate too much of.

"It's a balanced, nutritious meal in itself," Polly informed Crow.

"A balanced, nutritious meal in herself," he said, holding her around the waist and biting her neck.

Another present was helping him do all the dishes in the kitchen sink. It took an hour. Crow discovered the potato peeler he'd thought was lost forever.

"You don't need to give me things," he told her. "Just waking up every morning and thinking of you — it's Christmas."

"You shouldn't tell me things like that."

"Why not?" He pushed his dishwater-steamed glasses up his nose. "Why not?"

"If you don't know —"

But he put a hand over her mouth. "No, really."

"You should learn not to say everything that comes into your head. You should learn discretion."

"I can't, Polly, even if I wanted to, not with you. Are you a witch? Do you slip me truth serum when I'm not looking? Every thought I have when I'm with you, it goes *whoosh* . . ." He drew a hand from his heart, up his chest, and out his mouth. "Completely bypasses the brain."

"Very dangerous."

"Why?"

She couldn't remember, when he was looking at her like that.

He would have given her a present every day, if she'd let him. One afternoon on the way to his house the sky opened, and within seconds they were both drenched. They ran, holding hands, their jeans heavy, puddles in their shoes, hair stuck to their cheeks — kisses had a copper-penny taste in the rain, they discovered. At his house Crow gave her an old pair of his pants, and a shirt; she went into the bathroom and changed. The pants drooped, the shirt flopped, and the sun came out. Polly went out into the garden, where the colors of the earth and leaves had deepened, and where Crow took her picture without her knowing. Then he dried her hair. She didn't know about the photo till he handed it to her a week later. She was still wearing his shirt, which smelled of sweat and Ivory soap.

"You look like a child." He gazed over her shoulder.

"Yuck," she said, looking at herself. "Who wants to look like a child at the age of sixteen?"

"I guess I mean the wonder in your face."

Some nights when she couldn't fall asleep she turned on the light and looked at the photo, trying to see what he saw.

More and more when she couldn't fall asleep, it was from thinking of him. More and more, when she let her mind float, and one image after another rose to the surface, it was Crow's face she saw. Or his hands, the way in the sunlight the veins stood out on their backs like little rivers, the way they gently tamped down the soil around a seedling, or reached for her face. He held her face between his hands when he kissed her, and often when she got home and looked in the mirror, she would see the earth smudges on her cheeks, as if she herself were a seedling.

"Companion planting," he said. "The lettuce in the shade of the sweet corn. The basil protecting the tomatoes. If we were plants, don't you think we'd do well side by side?"

They didn't make love. Sometimes, as they walked to his house after school, his house that was always empty, Polly knew it was in both their minds. They swung their arms, fingers brushing; she slipped a sprig of forsythia in his buttonhole, and there, it hung between them, an unspoken question. But when they got to his house they always marched straight through it, through the grimy yellow kitchen and out the back door, to the garden. They walked past his room quickly, without looking at it, as if it embarrassed them, the way people hurry by two lovers on a beach, or a blind man begging. Crow was so shy, he didn't even like to kiss her when anyone could see.

He plants his kisses, Polly thought, looking out her bedroom window. One by one he drops them, or sometimes he scatters them, kisses too many and too small to count, like the seeds of parsley and thyme. And then he looks in my eyes as if he's waiting to see them bloom . . .

The phone made her jump.

"Hello?"

"Hi, babe."

"Oh. Hi, Boom."

"Whew, don't sound too excited."

"I've been meaning to talk to you."

"You could've fooled me. I got the impression you were trying to avoid me as much as humanly possible."

"Things have been happening."

"I know. You've been playing farmer-in-the-dell every afternoon."

"Very funny."

"That's okay. I don't have any claims on you. You can go here and there, as the crow flies."

"If I didn't know you better, I'd guess you were jealous."

"If I didn't know you better, I'd guess you were serious about him."

"Serious! You know I never get serious. You've got me breaking out in hives three inches high, just at the mention of the word."

"Okay, okay. I was just checking. Listen, I've got a crowd of people here, waiting for my leadership — you wouldn't be interested in going roller-skating, would you?"

"Not really."

"Me either, but I have a duty to my followers. I just

thought I'd call and let you know — I'm always around, babe, like the very air you breathe. In case you should ever decide to grace me with your presence."

"My presents?"

But he had already hung up.

She went back to the rocker by the window. Next to Naomi's begonia was the African violet Crow had given her. It was covered with white flowers and, despite Naomi's fears, it was doing well. Flourishing, almost. The next day, she thought, I bought him his hat. I haven't seen him without it since. I wonder if he wears it to bed.

The thought of Crow asleep, black hair falling into his eyes, made Polly smile. She rocked herself gently. I never get serious; she'd been meaning to tell Crow that for a while now. But, somehow, she never found the right moment.

The next afternoon, after they finished in the garden, he gave her her first recorder lesson. He showed her how to hold the wooden instrument; he took each of her fingers and placed it in the correct position. When she got tired of making tuneless toots he played for her. In the open air the sound seemed the closest a poor old human could get to birdsong. "Crow, you've turned into a nightingale!" Warning him she never got serious completely slipped her mind.

Chapter Nineteen

"I cannot believe it. I just cannot believe it."

Naomi was talking to herself as she strode down the hall, and she didn't care who heard her. She was wearing Danny's favorite jumper, his favorite shirt, his favorite earrings, his favorite perfume — and sweatsocks and sneakers. Someone had stolen her brand-new sandals, the ones her mother just bought her for Easter, out of her gym locker.

Last night Danny had called to ask her to go to Steer Inn with him today. This morning Naomi had dressed as if she were receiving the Nobel Prize. Now she looked like one of those women who hang around bus stations asking for a quarter.

"They cannot have been stolen," said Miss Hoop, her gym teacher, gazing placidly at Naomi through small, makeupless eyes.

"What do you mean?" exclaimed Naomi, holding up her bare foot as evidence, exhibit A. "They're stolen, my new sandals. My mother will kill me."

"You must not have locked your locker; therefore, you lost them, they are not stolen," Miss Hoop said.

The woman should get a job repossessing furniture or evicting old people from their homes, Naomi thought; she had just the right level of compassion. Naomi stared at the feet of all the girls who walked by. Hopeless, of course. She would never get her sandals back. That didn't even bother her as much as having Danny see her like this.

She could hardly sleep last night. This morning she'd gotten up an hour early to get ready. All through shorthand, while Mrs. Leech's dictation raced just out of reach of her pen, she imagined how he would say, "I've had a lot of time to think, Naomi, these endless days and nights apart from you, and I find I just can't live without . . ."

He was talking to Marcia Melon. Naomi saw them through the glass front doors. They sat side by side on the concrete ledge that rimmed some scraggly shrubs, Marcia Melon swinging her feet, which wore sandals exactly like Naomi's. Except that Naomi could never have squeezed her foot into one of Marcia's sandals. Everything about Marcia was small and soft and round, like a kitten. Or a rotten potato.

The Cinderella Effect again. Naomi concentrated on the Stamp Club's showcase display.

Marcia simpered away at last. As if someone had called, "Next!" Naomi pushed open the front door.

"Hi."

"Hi, Naomi."

He didn't seem to notice her jock feet. Was that a bad or a good sign?

"Donny wants me to work this afternoon, so I can't go to Steer Inn."

"That's okay. I'm on that diet, anyway." For you.

"Naomi, I wanted to talk to you."

"I know. You said."

"I have something important to say."

"All right."

"I've been doing a lot of thinking . . ."

"Uh-huh."

She focused on the shrubs behind him, where two empty beer bottles and a million cigarette butts lay in the dirt. Now is the moment. She fixed her eyes on the Molson bottle. She heard him draw his breath.

"And I think it's only fair to tell you, considering our past relationship, that I'm going out with somebody else."

At that moment in Naomi's woods a hepatica unfurled its silky blue petals for the first time; at that moment Mrs. Quinn muttered over a seventh-grade spelling test. A cod laid its nine millionth egg of the year; Polly invited Crow home for dinner. The earth hurtled through unimaginable black space, past exploding stars, dark stars, binary stars that revolved around each other, and Mrs. Denning's choco-nougat cake turned coal black as she wrote the paychecks for Ace Dry

Cleaners. At that moment Naomi realized that the person you loved could tell you, in a carefully rehearsed speech, that he was through with you, and you wouldn't die. You could go on standing there in his favorite dress and your smelly sweatsocks and you could say, "Oh. I'm glad you told me."

Chapter Twenty

Homeroom

Dear Nome,

Last night BBB called me and asked me to the prom. "Prom?" I said. "What's a prom?" He said I didn't appreciate what a compromise of his principles he was making, asking me over and over. Of course he was laughing, but something in his voice made me wonder — do you suppose even Boom Boom has a weak spot? In his heart, I mean — I know he has one in his head. It makes you wonder . . .

I tried to call you last night but your mother said you were upstairs. Did I detect a note of tension in her voice? How is Peter? How is Tess? How is Nome?

me

1st per.

Polly —

I used to think you went out with Boom Boom because you knew he must have a softness in him someplace and you wanted to try and get at it. I stopped thinking that a while ago, but maybe that's what you mean?

Peter is very fine. I'm doing some typing for him. My

mother is convinced we are having a mad love affair, especially since Tess is hardly ever home anymore, especially since anyone can see how irresistibly attractive I am and what a sex maniac Peter is. Anyway I am in love with fish. I will bore your head off about marine biology any time you have a minute. Which isn't too often lately I notice but believe me I understand.

On to Mrs. Rugchild and the wonderful world of history.

N.

second period

Dear Nome,

I forgot to tell you — I'm bringing Crow home to dinner. A command performance. Catherine is getting curious. "Crow?" she says, "Crow Stephens? I thought that boy's name was Jonathon! Bring him home — you know I always like to see my old students!" Poor Crow. "I'll do it, for you," he says, as if he's going before a firing squad. I thought of all kinds of excuses to give my mother, but then I decided, I can't protect him from everything. My mother's just a person, after all, not a fire-breathing dragon. And Crow can't go through the rest of his life hiding out from things that scare him. Right?

Poor Nome — when I saw you just now you looked like something the cat forgot to bury. I'll cheer you up at lunch!

Polly,

Thanks for the compliment.

Maybe you can't go through life hiding out. But right now what I think I'd like more than anything would be to live the rest of my life on a dessert island. I'd eat pineapples and drink cold water, and I'd be very skinny and very wise, and even if I was lonely so what. At least there'd be nobody to hurt me. You can't hurt yourself.

I think I'll skip lunch — I'm not hungry.

Dear dear Nome,

Maybe you can hurt yourself. It's something I've been wondering about lately.

I wish I knew how to make you feel better.

Love,
me

P.S. *Desert* island.

Chapter Twenty-one

"Oh wow, look at this!" Cass came hurtling in from the mailbox, waving a piece of paper. "From the Happy Lad Baking Company!"

"Let me see that." Mrs. Quinn took the paper from her. Last week Cass had found a wrinkle of plastic, a little shred of polyethylene, embedded in her Happy Lad Cream-Filled Cupcake, and Mrs. Quinn had written the company an irate letter. "'This coupon good for ten packages of Happy Lad Cream-Filled Cupcakes,'" she read out now.

"Oh wow," cried Cass, turning a cartwheel. "I lo-ove those cupcakes."

"A bribe." Mrs. Quinn tore the coupon in half.

"Mom!" Cass wailed in disbelief.

"No letter, no apology, no explanation. It's a bribe, out-and-out. Well, Happy Lads, you are about to hear from Catherine Quinn again."

Cass tried to fit the halves back together. "Couldn't we complain *and* keep the coupon?"

"No we could not," replied her mother, hauling out her typewriter.

"But why?"

"Because, Cass, it is the principle of the thing that matters."

"Principle schminciple." Cass regarded the torn coupon sadly. "It was just a tiny bit of plastic, you know."

"There's no telling what it might be next time. The point is, the company is guilty of gross negligence, and rather than account for themselves they're trying to bribe their way off the hook. People are too willing to swallow — literally — this kind of thing. No wonder the world is in the state it is."

"So who cares about the world."

"Don't pester me, Cass. I must think."

Cass moped into the kitchen, where Polly, her hair wound around electric rollers, was peeling potatoes. Crow was coming to dinner that night. "How come Mommy likes to fight with people?"

"She's just standing up for her rights, Cass."

"She likes to fight," Cass repeated, tossing the coupon into the garbage. "It's always gotta be her against somebody. Sometimes I think she's a real retard."

Crow arrived exactly on time, wearing, beneath his down jacket, a blue shirt, a navy blue tie with red stripes, and a sports coat whose sleeves were too short. Polly had brushed out her hair and changed into a pale green shirt with wide lace cuffs. When she kissed him she got a whiff of mothballs and alcohol-y aftershave; his glasses steamed up in the warm foyer.

"You look pretty," he said.

"So do you."

"I bought a tie to impress you."

"I'm impressed."

"Only then I remembered I didn't have a tie clasp, so I had to wear this." It was a gold-plated bulldog with a red glass eye. "I gave it to my father for his birthday a long time ago," he said, giving it a dubious look.

She took him by the hand and led him into the living room, where her mother was tapping out the final draft of her letter. A pencil clenched between her teeth, her face was one big frown. Crow hid behind Polly as she said, "Mom. Mom!"

Mrs. Quinn blinked, looked up. Before she could say a word, or bite him, Crow reached around Polly and held out a bouquet wrapped in green tissue paper.

"Well, thank you," said Mrs. Quinn, taking the pencil from between her teeth. "Thank you very much, Jonathon," she said, craning her neck to see around Polly.

"You're welcome."

Polly was afraid he would bow. Instead, he nodded his head stiffly.

"Well, Jonathon, it's been a few years since I've seen you, hasn't it? I won't say you've grown because you know that better than anyone. Well, how nice." She peeked inside the paper. "Tulips, lovely. Polly, how about the yellow vase? Wouldn't they look nice in that?"

"I'll get it."

Crow started to follow Polly out to the kitchen, but Mrs. Quinn tapped his arm, freezing him in his tracks. "Tell me something, if you will," she said, leaning toward him. "There's something that has me puzzled. Polly tells me you're called Crow. Now why on earth do people call you that when you have a fine name like Jonathon?"

He brushed the hair from his eyes, shifted from one foot to another. "Because I have such a big nose?" he guessed.

"It's just a nickname," Polly called from the dining room. "People've called him that since grade school."

"But you don't like it much," stated Mrs. Quinn.

"Not much." He tugged on the sleeves on his jacket.

"Then you should correct people. Intelligent people don't mind correction. Jonathon is a fine name, and you look much more like a Jonathon than a Crow to me."

"Thank you," he said uncertainly.

"Come and eat!"

Polly had set the table with their best dishes, silver, and had even bought candles. She put the tulips in the center of the table. Crow, used to eating from a pan, leaning against the stove, looked a little dazed by it all. He sat where Polly told him to and obediently ate whatever she put on his plate: corned beef, cabbage, new potatoes with parsley, hot fluffy biscuits. But the conversation had a little trouble getting started. Cass, sitting beside him, pushing biscuits into her mouth, didn't take her eyes off him. Buttering her fourth biscuit, she said, "I like your tie clasp."

"Thank you."

"You got any cleats?"

"No, sorry."

"Too bad, mine rolled down the sewer drain. You sure you don't even got one? Boom Boom's got loads."

A boiled potato rolled off Crow's fork and onto the rug.

"Boom Boom has many," said Mrs. Quinn. "Stop filling up on biscuits and eat your cabbage, Cass."

"I hate cabbage."

"Crow's growing his own cabbage, Mom," said Polly, glowering at Cass and spooning more of it onto her plate.

"Really! That's right — you're the one Polly's planting a garden with, aren't you. Tell me this — how do you handle cabbage worms? Every time I've tried to grow cabbage the little devils eat more of it than I do."

At last Crow had something to talk about. Laying down his fork, he explained how he dusted the cabbages with flour early in the morning, when they were still wet with dew, and how when the sun came up the flour hardened, trapping the worms and killing them. "There's also a way," he said, "of grinding the worms up into a paste. They say if you smear that on the cabbage leaves, the moths won't lay their eggs there."

"Ooooh, nasty! Ground-up worms, ooh, ugh!" Cass doubled over, clutching her stomach. "Now I can't eat my cabbage, Mommy. He made me nauseous."

Her mother gave her what her students called the Look. "*Nauseated*. And I suppose that means you don't want any dessert, either?"

"I never ground up the worms myself, actually," Crow said in a low voice, looking at his plate. "I just read you could."

"It sounds like a very good idea," Mrs. Quinn assured him. "All-natural, right, Polly? I'll have to try it. All right, Cassiopeia, take just one bite — that's it — oh, what a face! Careful or it'll freeze that way! All right, you've earned your pie."

Polly cleared the dishes and brought in a lemon meringue

pie and a pot of tea. After devouring two enormous pieces Cass excused herself from the table and reappeared a moment later holding the recorder Crow had lent Polly.

"Would you mind playing this for me? I'd like to hear what it's supposed to sound like. I *know* it's not supposed to sound the way it does when Polly plays it."

"The music critic."

"Come on, would ya?" wheedled Cass. "Play 'Part-time Lover.'"

"Oh, I can't play that on a recorder," said Crow. "I don't think —"

"Now don't be modest with us, Jonathon. Polly told us what an accomplished player you are."

Crow brushed the hair from his eyes, buttoned and unbuttoned his jacket. "I can't . . ."

"Just one song."

"Maybe just one? The one you played in the garden the other day?"

Crow didn't know how to say no to Polly. "Well, you asked for it. You can hold your ears if they start to hurt."

"Come on."

He played the song that was Polly's favorite, the soft, low, melancholy one that made her think of roses turning brown, fading photographs, women pacing the shore waiting for lovers who would never return. The song rose and fell like breath itself, and Polly found she couldn't look at him while he played. She looked at the candles, the tulips, the shadows the crumbs cast on the tablecloth, at the glisten of the white-gold pie. If she looked up now all she felt would well up and spill over, and everyone would see . . .

"What was the name of that piece?" Mrs. Quinn's voice was husky. Polly looked up in surprise. In the candlelight her mother's face was soft.

"I'm not sure of the name," he said. "It's an old Irish folk song. I . . . I learned it for Polly."

"Aah. I thought so. You don't remember it, Polly?"

"Remember it?"

"How did the words go? 'I wish my love was a red rose, and bloomed in yon garden fair.' You don't remember? Your father used to sing it."

"Oh."

Crow took the recorder apart and began vigorously drying it out with the tip of his tie.

"The rest was, oh . . . can I remember?" Mrs. Quinn closed her eyes. "Something about wishing to be a butterfly, or a nightingale. 'And year by year I'd love my dear, let the wind blow high or low.' Yes, that was it."

They all sat without speaking, till Cass slid around the table and put her head on her mother's shoulder. "Don't be sad, Mommy."

Mrs. Quinn opened her eyes. "Sad? I'm not sad, treasure." She smiled and rumpled Cass's hair, to prove it. "A slight touch of the self-pity-itis, that's all. Nothing fatal. Music is a dangerous weapon, Jonathon — be careful how you use it."

"Yes," he said.

"You play very well. Don't put yourself down. Never hide your light." With that she switched on the dining-room chandelier, making them all blink. "I have papers to grade — no, let me unset, Polly. You made a lovely dinner." Mrs. Quinn stacked the dessert dishes, then turned to Crow. "You must come again, Jonathon. And good luck with your garden, and the war against worms. By the way, how on earth did you get Polly interested in gardening? Whenever I try to enlist her help around here, she moans, 'It's so bor-r-ring.'"

Crow grinned, blushed. Mrs. Quinn gave him a wink and pushed through the swinging door into the kitchen.

"She was sad, wasn't she?" asked Cass softly, looking at Polly.

"I don't know."

"Music can do that to people," said Crow.

"It was more than just the music." Cass gave a slow shake of her head. "She was sad. Real sad. 'Cause of our father. How come Mommy doesn't mind being mad but she doesn't like to be sad?"

"I don't know," Polly said again. From the kitchen came the sound of dishes being briskly scraped.

"Hey, Cass," said Crow, "how'd you like a present? It's not as good as a cleat, but you can have it if you want it." And unclasping the bulldog from his tie, he held it out to her.

Cass's face lit up, then turned dubious. She knows, Polly thought; she knows it's a bribe not to feel bad about her parents, a bribe just as surely as the cupcake coupon was. And for a moment she watched Cass hesitate between clinging to her sorrow, and letting it be soothed away. Cass hesitated — but not very long. All at once she reached out and snatched the comfort that was within her reach.

"Thanks," she said, "a lot."

From the kitchen came the rumble and *whoosh* of the dishwasher being turned on.

"I guess I should go," said Crow.

"I'll walk you to the corner."

Outside Crow unzipped his jacket and pulled off his tie. The night was clear, the stars crystal chips; the Big Dipper was upside down, as if hurled up there by some tipsy giant. Polly walked Crow to the corner and farther, past the spook house, out of Laughing Brooks and into Naomi's neighborhood.

"It wasn't too bad, was it?"

"I like your sister."

"And my mother?"

"She's complicated."

"She's a strong woman."

"I guess she's had to be, whether she wanted to or not."

In the upstairs window of the Denning house, Polly saw Naomi and Peter looking at a book together. Naomi sat at a table and Peter stood beside her, leaning one hand on the table, gesturing with the other. He was talking, and Naomi was staring raptly at his pointing finger.

They circled around and came back to the spook house, which looked more ominous than ever, home to no one but mice and spiders.

"Here's our house, Polly." Holding hands, they ducked beneath the beech tree's low, sweeping branches. Facing her, leaning his shoulder against the smooth silver bark, Crow traced the outlines of her face with his fingers.

"This is our place," he whispered to her, "where we can come and get away from everything. We don't have to think about anyone or anything else. It's just us, just you and me." He unbuttoned her coat and touched her here, there, gently, while he kissed her. "Just you and me," he said, holding her face between his hands. His kisses drew something out of her, something bittersweet as the flute song. She felt it rising up in her, a mixture of longing and fear. For one moment what he said was true: Nothing existed but this tree, this living house, and the two of them . . .

And then she began to feel cold. "I have to go."

He wanted to walk her back home, but she said she wanted to be alone now. "I want to think. Sometimes being with you is like having so many presents heaped on me, I can't take it all in."

He kissed her once more.

She walked home slowly, rebuttoning her coat against the night air. Naomi and Peter were gone from the window, but the light still burned there. At home Cass was in the bathtub, splashing and singing at the top of her lungs, " 'Lovin' somebody, it's a full-time job . . .' " Her mother sat at her desk, the typewriter back in its case, the Happy Lad letter neatly addressed and stamped, a crisp white rectangle of indignation. She looked up from her pile of test papers when Polly came in.

"Well?" asked Polly. "What did you think?"

"Is he that afraid of everyone, or is it just me?"

"He's shy."

"I like him. I sense some gumption in him, underneath."

"You have to get to know him." Polly hung up her coat. "That's what I told him about you, too."

Mrs. Quinn made a face. "And what are his plans for the future?"

"He's not sure. He thinks about going to college, or music school, but he doesn't have much money."

"In that case, please have him to dinner again, but tell him to skip the flowers. He ought to be saving his money, not spending it on tulips. He can't eat tulips." She took up her red pen.

"No, he can't."

Polly went down the hall, past the closed bathroom door to the linen closet, where she slipped out a photo album with a plaid cloth cover. She shut the door of her room, sat in the rocker by the window, and opened the album.

On the first page was the photo of her mother and father sitting on a beach, toes in the sand, her father tousle-headed, her mother with her knees drawn up to her chin, smiling broadly, forgetting or not caring about her bad front teeth. Then the wedding picture: Catherine prim and beautiful in a dark suit with a bunch of artificial cherries pinned to it, gripping her bouquet and looking straight out at the photographer, while her handsome, rumpled new husband gazed down at her with bewildered joy.

On the next page the photos of Polly started: Polly at two, held above her father's head like a trophy; at three on a sled with him, so bundled up she looked like a sleeping bag with a face pasted on, he bareheaded and grinning. The album's pages were brittle, their corners bent, and Polly turned them carefully. She and her father were sitting on the steps of a house she didn't recognize, both in bathing suits, hers with a white skirt and an anchor on the chest. Her father rested his cheek on his palm, looking down at her.

He looked as if he loved her. Loved them both. For the first time Polly felt sorry for her father. There must have been times he regretted what he'd done. Many times, maybe. Lonely nights, mornings when he woke from dreams of them — and what did he do then? Sing?

Happily ever after — your father never admitted that only happens in fairy tales and movies.

Sitting there, curly wet hair, smiling down at her. Thinking . . . what? Not of leaving, not just then. The house behind them was shingled in tar paper. Beneath the photo, in white ink, Catherine had written, "Bathing beauties — the house on Jones Street." That was in another town, another life, a tumbledown rented house.

Then Polly knew why she had that feeling whenever she turned down Crow's street. Once she, her mother, and her father had lived in a house something like his.

"I said, 'Lovin' somebody is a full-time job!'"

"Cass, get out of that tub before you shrink!"

Her mother came down the hall, went into her room, opened her closet door. Polly knew she was laying out her clothes for school tomorrow, the way she did every night.

He can't eat tulips. Can we eat roses?

Polly turned the pages, but there were no photos of her father with his arms full of roses. There was one of Polly on her first day of school, braids tied with satin bows, and one of her father outside a church, holding Cassiopeia Ann Quinn in a long white christening dress. And then the photos abruptly stopped, leaving two or three blank black pages. There was a large gap in the Quinn family album. The next pictures were of Polly at twelve and Cass at five, and they were in a different album, one with a vinyl cover and plastic-wrapped pages.

Polly took the photo of her and her father in bathing suits out of the album and put it in the drawer of her night table, along with the one Crow had taken of her. She slipped the album back in place on the closet shelf, then went to unload the dishwasher. On the dining-room table, between the candles, she saw that the red tulips had begun to gently unfold their petals.

Chapter Twenty-two

"You're going upstairs *again?*"

"I'm doing typing for him," Naomi told her mother. "It's almost the end of the semester, and he has a couple of big projects due. He pays me." A slight kink in the truth —

once Peter had said he'd hire her, someday, as his assistant famous biologist.

"He can afford to pay you for typing, with his rent two weeks overdue?"

"Things are a little tight for him now. You know, since Tess moved out, he has to pay the whole rent himself, instead of just half." She felt like an interpreter, running messages between upstairs and down. How could her mother even think about the rent money — didn't she see what a petty thing that was, compared to being abandoned by a lover? "I know he'll pay it as soon as he can."

"And that's what you do up there — type?" Mrs. Denning was, after all, not only concerned about the money.

"Of course, can't you hear me?" When Naomi was up at Peter's she pounded on the typewriter at regular intervals. Peter didn't even blink when she jumped up from her book, or the TV (the educational channel), or the table where they were dunking Twinkies in milk — he didn't raise an eyebrow when she suddenly went to the typewriter and thundered out ten lines of *q*'s. Nor did he notice how careful she was he didn't sit in the swing and thump, thus giving her mother the Wrong Idea. Peter was still in a daze. Trivialities were obscured.

Though he had noticed her perfume last night. Jasmine, she told him. *Jasminum fruticans,* he qualified, consulting a book of botany.

"Yes, I hear you. But every day for a week is too much, Naomi. How do you know you're not making a nuisance of yourself?"

"He's lonely."

"I'm sure he is." Mrs. Denning's brows rushed together. "That's what worries me."

The phone rang. Naomi raced to get it. It was Polly.

"Want to go to the mall? Or anyplace? The vacation's almost over, and we haven't done anything together."

Naomi would much rather have gone upstairs. But something in Polly's voice made her say, "Okay, I'll be right over."

She told her mother, who said, "Thank goodness." She ran up to tell Peter, who was mopping up a Sugar Smacks variety pack that had self-destructed. "Can I bring you anything from the mall?"

"Would you mind picking up a pack of graph paper?"

"I don't mind."

"I don't know what I'd do without you, Macaroni."

What would I do without good old Nome, thought Polly, hanging up. I can always count on her. I have to get out of this house n-o-w.

All week, the entire spring vacation, Polly had stayed home. Crow was working at Wally's. Atwater had offered him extra hours, and Polly told him to take them. "You could use the money," she said. "Shove the money," he said, "I want to be with you. I want to spend a whole day with you — I want to watch the sun rise with you, and . . ." "The sun will always be there," she said, "and I won't disappear. Sometimes I think you're afraid the minute I'm out of your sight I'll disappear." He said, "I am afraid of that, can't you tell?"

The days of that week, the last week of April, had melted one into the other, as Polly sat out in her back yard, not reading the book on her knees, not threading the embroidery needle between her fingers. "Woo, you're spacey," Cass said, "really spacey." Polly remembered what she'd felt when her breasts first began to swell and change. Wonder and fear, joy and anger — it was happening to her, it was inevitable, one Polly was giving way to another, and there was nothing she could do about it. Now, sitting there in the back yard, she knew again that jumble of feelings. Her mother's lilies were out. Crow said the peas were blooming, white flowers flecked with gold. She had to come see. "I don't *have* to," she teased.

Last night they had gone to a movie at his father's theater. Mr. Stephens, met at last, was an old Crow — tall, thin, soft-spoken. He sat in his office eating a prune Danish, and when they came in he stood up and the Danish went skidding off his lap and into the wastebasket. The movie was awful, about girls in a boarding school who were always getting into mischief. The theater was a small, independent one, and couldn't afford to bid on the big-name films. "Grade Z," Polly told Crow, who looked hurt. "Not you, the movie," she said, laughing.

This morning she remembered that look on his face, and felt a tinge of impatience. She'd just washed her hair; she sat on the front steps, combing it out. It was an overcast day, damp, the kind of day when fool's gold looks like just that. Mrs. Quinn, on vacation, was mowing the back lawn, which didn't need it; Polly could hear the close-cut grass cry, *Ouch!* The vacation was nearly over; where had it gone? Dreamed away. "What'd you do over vacation?" everyone would be asking on Monday. "Nothing," she'd have to say. "I contemplated my navel." "You? Polly Quinn?"

Just then Boom Boom flew in, *va-room*. He was piloting a copper-colored 747, with plush gold interior. Polly walked slowly to the curb. Danny, Marcia Melon, and Tom DeMillo were in the back seat. The front seat beside Boom Boom was empty, except for three six-packs of beer. He was wearing his baseball cap with the visor turned around catcher-style, and a

T-shirt that said TO KNOW ME IS TO LOVE ME. When he leaned over to turn down the radio, Polly saw that he already had the beginnings of a tan; it started just below his sleeve, just above the biceps. By the end of the summer he would look like the guy who kicks sand in the weakling's face in body-building ads. He leaned his elbow on the open window, his chin on his fist, gave her his Joe Namath smile.

"Hi, stranger."

Polly thought, Does he expect me to faint dead away now? "Hi yourself."

"Hi, Polly," cooed Marcia Melon, in cutoffs and a halter, from the back seat. Danny nodded stiffly, then became intensely interested in the dome light. At least he was decent enough to be embarrassed. Tom DeMillo bobbed his head at her, or in time with the radio, it was hard to tell which.

"Partying at this hour of the morning?" Polly asked.

"We're driving out to Pumpkin Notch. There's a big party out there today. Parking Lot Ten."

"I heard something about that party."

"Music, food, a little of this, a little of that —"

"All right!" cried Tom DeMillo. "Let's go!"

"Sounds like fun," said Polly, using her comb to pull a tangle of hair around before her face.

Boom Boom patted the soft gold seat between him and the beer. "Well?"

She examined the snarl in her hair, bringing it up close to her eyes. "Boom, has it ever crossed your mind that there might be more to life than partying?"

He pushed the cap back on his head. "Uh-oh, she wants to get philosophical. Okay. In answer to your question, Yes it has crossed my mind. It has also crossed my mind that since no one knows what's going to happen tomorrow, we might as well party while we can. To wit, the hedonist philosophy. We find more modern echoes of it in the existentialists, who say that man is what he chooses, and so —"

"See, that's the thing about you, Boom Boom. You're not stupid. You just pretend to be."

In the back seat Marcia Melon tittered and Danny began to investigate the electric window. Boom Boom's grin dared Polly to go on. His smugness, his handsomeness, her own boredom — she couldn't resist saying, "Sometimes I think you see yourself in one of those dramas where one actor plays all the parts. You're as confused as that fish Nome told me about, the one that's always changing its color and sex." She threw a look at Danny, who closed his thumb in the electric window. "And another thing I've been meaning to ask you: When are you going to stop calling yourself Boom Boom? Don't you think it's a slightly ridiculous name for an eighteen-year-old? What are you smiling at?"

He lifted his chin from his palm. "You, babe."

"Will you stop calling me 'babe'? And what do you mean?"

"Think about it. Better yet, come along and we'll discuss it." Again he patted the seat beside him.

"What is this, 'Days of Our Lives'?" complained Tom from the back seat. "'As the World Turns'? The beer's getting warm! Come on, let's go!"

Marcia Melon sat on the edge of the seat, hands clasped between her knees, hanging on their every word. She'd give anything, Polly thought, to be sitting in the front seat; on a scale of one to ten, Boom Boom's a ten, Danny maybe a six. She felt an urge to say okay and jump in the car, just to make that moon-eyed Marcia jealous. People were probably already beginning to show up at Pumpkin Notch, but the party wouldn't really start till Boom Boom got there.

Polly saw herself in her new embroidered skirt, sipping from his beer, saw herself wading into the icy surf, clinging to his arm, saw . . .

Boom Boom raced the motor. "My father makes me buy the gas, you know. Your indecision's getting expensive here."

"And the beer's getting warm," wailed Tom, reaching over the seat and patting the bottles.

"I have things to do today," Polly said. "Though I might consider continuing this conversation some other time."

"I don't know, babe. There's a limit to even my super-human patience." He shifted the car into gear, looked straight at her. "Don't count on me when you get tired of him."

He roared away from the curb, throwing Tom backward into his seat. As they tore away Polly heard the radio flipped up high again.

> *There's givin' and there's takin' love,*
> *They're just two sides of makin' love,*
> *I don't want . . .*

She shook her head, going back up the front walk. Old Boom Boom. She went inside and got the shirt she was making Crow, meaning to sit outside and work on it. But she kept pricking her fingers, the thread was in knots, and she threw it down. She went out to the garage and looked at the desk from Trash 'n' Treasures she meant to refinish — looked at it, and wandered away. She picked up a book and put it down; she rolled a sheet of paper into her type-writer and took it out.

The thought of Boom Boom and that party was like a sliver beneath her skin. Crazy old 3B with his hat and his tan and his grin. "Count on you?" she should have demanded. "I'd count on there being a Santa Claus before I'd count on you." Boom would have had a good comeback. Marcia Melon would have turned green.

Crow was so serious. Probably that was why, no matter how often he reminded her, she kept on calling him Crow instead of Jonathon. She wanted to keep one silly thing about him. Even if he weren't working now, he wouldn't have wanted to go to the beach party. He didn't like parties. And if she'd been able to drag him there, he'd probably have wanted to go off for a long walk, holding her hand to make sure she didn't disappear, just the two of them, so he wouldn't have to feel shy, so he wouldn't have to worry about someone else catching her eye . . .

"Nome? Want to go to the mall? Or anyplace?"

They walked there, along the highway, past Wally's. Through the window they saw Crow pricing cans, but he didn't see them, and Polly didn't want to go in.

In the mall the windows were full of summer clothes, Styrofoam suns and plastic flowers. Everyone was there, everyone who wasn't at Pumpkin Notch: strolling back and forth, sitting on the rim of the fountain, leaning against the snack bar. Naomi bought the graph paper and then they sat on the edge of a small pool, its bottom spattered with pennies and ancient chewing gum.

Now Naomi told Polly, "Tess has left Peter."

"Oh no!"

"Oh yes. A week ago, just before vacation started."

"And you didn't tell me?"

"I haven't seen you."

"That's true."

"What have you been up to?"

"I was asking myself the same question this morning." Polly tossed back her hair. "But tell me about Peter and Tess."

"It was awful to watch. Of course I couldn't help watching, from the dining-room window. They went up and down the back stairs I don't know how many times, carrying out her stuff — records, art supplies, the toaster —"

"He helped her?"

"Of course he helped her. She had a lot of stuff and you know how little and skinny she is." Naomi sighed, the way she always did at the thought of someone slender.

"I know, but it seems too rational. You'd think he'd have thrown her stuff down the stairs."

"They're not like that. They never yell or get mad. They discuss; they try to get to the root of things. They have a very organic relationship."

A little boy ran up the bridge that spanned the pool. He stuck out his tongue at his mother, who stood helpless, her arms full of packages.

"Arnold! Come to Mommy this minute."

"Na na, na na!"

"It sounds as if you know a lot about Tess and Peter's relationship."

"Well, I've been going up there a lot. Every night, as a matter of fact, and Peter . . . he tells me things." Naomi examined the bag with the graph paper in it. "We really talk to each other sometimes. I even told him a little about Danny."

"You did?" Polly thought of Danny and Marcia Melon in the back seat of Boom Boom's car, and wondered if she should tell Naomi. "You talked to him about that?"

"I'm counting to three, Arnold. One . . ."

"We've helped each other. We're fellow rejects." Naomi gave a laugh that made Polly think of a teacup breaking.

"Two . . ."

"You can get used to it, you know. Being a reject." Naomi rolled and unrolled the the edge of the paper bag. "At first you go around feeling like a lump of cold mashed potatoes, but then slowly, so, so slowly . . . a whole minute goes by and you don't think of him. Then a half hour. One day a whole hour before some word or smell or song makes you remember, and down you go again. . . . It's been a relief, this week off, not having to see him with her."

So she already knew.

"Two and three-quarters . . ."

"Anyway, I watched Peter drive Tess away, and he didn't come back till late that night. And then — oh, Polly!"

"What, Nome?"

"When he finally did come back — you know their bedroom is right over mine — well, I could hear him crying."

"Oh no."

"It just about killed me. I never heard anything so sad. I knew just how he felt."

"Three! That's it, Arnold!"

"You can't get me, you can't get me!"

Naomi stood up, whirled around, and shouted, "Arnold, get the hell off that bridge *now!*"

Arnold came down the bridge immediately, eyes abulge and mouth agape. His mother grabbed him and dragged him off down the mall without a backward glance, while the children who'd gathered to watch moved off in awed silence.

"The next day I went up and helped him plant an avocado," Naomi went on in her normal voice, sitting back down, ignoring Polly's wide eyes. "And I've been going up there ever since. The avocado's doing real good. He doesn't really have anyone besides me — most of his friends are his and Tess's friends, and he doesn't feel like seeing them."

"I guess not."

"I try to tell him you get used to it, and he tells me his mother always says, 'God save us from all the things we can get used to.'"

"It was good you broke up with Danny, Nome. He was starting to use you."

"Don't rub it in, okay?"

Polly blinked.

"We've sort of settled into a routine. I go up there after dinner — my mother rolls her eyes and mutters under her breath, she can't believe Tess left him, she always predicted it'd be the other way around — and we keep each other company. It's peaceful up there. We read. Every day I find out something new that just about stops my breath. Last night I was reading about the creatures that live in the deepest part of the ocean — a mile deeper than Mount Everest is tall. It's totally black down there, and freeeeeezing. Not to mention the incredibly high pressure of all that water. The most amazing creatures live there. There's a squid that's covered with hundreds of lights, all colors, and the squid can blink them on and off, one by one, with a little shutter of skin it pulls up or down. It's one of those things they can't explain exactly. There's no real need for so many lights and so many different colors — just like there's no real reason for the coral and anemones to be such beautiful colors. I like to think of that squid down there. The ink it shoots out is fire-colored."

"So he's really tutoring you in biology?" Realizing that could be taken two ways, Polly hid a smile.

"He's studying the sex life of animals without backbones."

"I beg your pardon." Polly thought it was time for a joke.

"You know, jellyfish, worms. Sponges? Our ancestors."

"Speak for yourself."

"Forget it, then," cried Naomi, standing up abruptly. For the second time in five minutes, Polly looked at her in astonishment. "Just forget it. I have to go, Peter needs this paper."

"Nome, don't get mad. I was only teasing!" Polly grabbed her elbow.

Naomi yanked it away and threw her arms wide. "You don't understand. Neither do I, that's the point. We go around with our eyes shut, not understanding half of what's going on around us. Or in us. All that life in the ocean. Did you ever dream of it? It's just like our bodies. All those little miracles going on constantly, our hearts beating and our lungs pumping and our blood racing round and round — do you ever think about it? Never mind try to *understand* it? Please don't look at me like I'm crazy. There's so much to know, it scares me. Peter keeps promising me the future is wide open, but I never thought I . . . Some days it's as if I have fountains splashing around inside me — will you stop looking at me like that? Those days I feel so good I want to grab people and shake them and say, 'How dare you look so bored and dull? Don't you know how wonderful everything is? Even the tiniest grain of sand?' But then, other days, oh . . ." Like a windup toy that had run down, Naomi collapsed beside Polly. "Other days the fountains get all clogged up, they can't get out and I feel so wretched, I think I've never felt more lonely . . ."

Polly touched her friend's hand. Fallen in love with Peter! Poor Nome.

Chapter Twenty-three

That night, after supper, Naomi climbed the back stairs to Peter's. The door was ajar; he knew she was coming. He lay on the floor, elbows propped on a pillow, lab notebook spread before him, a red-bearded island in a sea of debris. The apartment had become a disaster area. Naomi had to pick her way across an aromatic pile of laundry, a Count Chocula box, one empty and two half-full teacups, four crushed soda cans, and at least a dozen Twinkie wrappers (Peter had been on a junk-food binge since Tess left). She plucked a pair of socks out of what she'd come to think of as her chair, and draped them over *Construction #1,* the one thing Tess had left behind.

"Thanks for getting me the graph paper."

"You're welcome."

"I have a new book for you."

"Not a hard one?"

"It's time you graduated from picture books."

"But that's my speed! I love looking at all those amazing photographs — they make me feel . . . giddy. As opposed to looking at your organic chem book, which makes me feel like an imbecile."

"You could learn organic chem, if you set your mind to it."

"You're so big on the word 'could.'"

"And *you're* so good at fishing for compliments. Ho, a pun. Here, try this."

"Rachel Carson?"

"You'll like her. She's got the same instinct for beauty you do."

Naomi held the book up before her blooming face. She

read that around each individual grain of sand swam incomprehensibly small beings, all living, dying, feeding, reproducing — an entire world attached to each single particle of sand.

Naomi no longer asked Peter, "Are you making that up?"

From downstairs came the sound of her family's TV, with its sudden explosions of canned laughter. Her mother banged a pot; the back door opened and her father banged a garbage can. The sounds seemed to drift up from another world. It was so peaceful up here. She and Peter could sit for an hour without saying a word. None of those little alarms went off when she was with him. It was almost as easy as being alone.

The same instinct for beauty you do. Peter didn't say things just to be nice.

Naomi laid down Rachel Carson and sneaked out one of the picture books. She opened it at random. There was the fish that hung on the wall in the Hideaway. Only alive, glistening, flying through the air. "The sailfish," she read, "is the swiftest fish of all. It has been clocked at speeds up to 68 mph, and has been known to leap across 40 feet of water."

Naomi looked up. Peter was staring at *Construction #1,* his furry brown head in his hands. Everything began to crumble a little, around the edges.

"Got any Twinkies?" she asked, and he turned, smiled.

"Do fish have scales?"

As corny as her father. He stood up and stretched, his sweater riding up so she could see the curly hairs low on his chest, curls the same reddish color her cheeks turned at the sight.

"There is no such thing as a platonic relationship. That's my mother's latest pronouncement," she told him. "Thank you," she added, as he handed her her Twinkie on a chipped green plate.

"What brought that up?"

"I don't know," she lied. "My mother feels sorry for me, not having a boyfriend. I think she was getting a real varicose thrill out of it."

"You mean vicarious."

"Yeah. Anyway, now she keeps asking me if I want to have a party. Or if I want to have someone — read that someone male — over for dinner." Naomi broke her cake in half and regarded the filling.

"She's worried you'll turn out to be an old maid," Peter laughed.

Naomi didn't really think that was funny. "Well, she's probably right." She took a lick of filling. "I guess she just wants me to be happy."

"Sure she wants you to be happy. Only happiness doesn't come in one-size-fits-all. What've you been thinking about college?"

"Well, I thought I might go see my guidance counselor when school starts again. Of course he's about as much help as a two-year-old. Usually he gets me mixed up with somebody else. 'Hello there, Suzie!' he says. Or else he looks at my record, smiles, says he's sure I'll make a fine secretary, and zaps me right back to study hall."

"I remember what clowns those guys could be. Listen, Naomi, you have to start looking out for yourself. You have to start thinking of your future with a capital F."

Corny and grave as a father. Naomi smiled down at the crumbs in her lap. "Hmm," she said.

Outside a gentle rain began to fall. Peter sat in her chair, pulling on his pipe, and she sat at the card table, plodding through the shorthand due on Monday. He looked up suddenly and asked, "Do you know this town is in approximately the same latitude as Tashkent, Peking, and the ruins of Pompeii?"

"To tell you the truth, no."

"You should think of things like that once in a while." He was as big on "should" as "could."

Naomi put down what he called her hieroglyphics. "Peter, how about *I* show *you* something for a change. How'd you like to go to those woods I told you about?"

"That's a great idea. After this rain there should be some fungi around. I'd like to look at some fungi."

"We could go as soon as I get home from church, if the rain stops."

"I'll drive."

"I'll bring a picnic."

Naomi had trouble getting to sleep that night.

Chapter Twenty-four

The day broke soft and clear, the most lovely day yet that spring.

After church Naomi flung off her good clothes, pulled on her jeans, and rummaged around for a shirt. In her bottom drawer, stuffed in a corner, was the blue tangle of Danny's unfinished scarf. With a little pang Naomi pushed it farther back in the drawer, thinking maybe she'd give it to Polly, who might be able to make something of it. She pulled on a dark green T-shirt she didn't look too pudgy in, and studied herself in the mirror. Here I am, she thought. Here I am.

On the way to the kitchen she practiced telling her mother,

"I'm going out with Peter." Through the front windows came the steady whine of the power mower. Last night's rain had left everything lush and sparkling. Sun-day. In the kitchen, her chicken already in the oven, Mrs. Denning sat with her account books before her. As quietly as possible Naomi opened the refrigerator and began to fill a paper bag with apples, pears, and the week-old remains of her Easter candy. Mr. Denning still bought her a chocolate rabbit and jelly beans each year. It was no wonder *he* didn't worry about what Naomi did upstairs. Naomi had sometimes considered sending him a formal notice: Be it known henceforth: Your daughter Naomi is no longer a little girl!

Though she did love candy. And knew Peter did, too.

"What are you doing?"

"Oh, just going on a little picnic."

"A picnic?" Her mother laid down her pencil. "Who are you going with?"

She hopes I'll say Danny. Naomi popped a jelly bean — ten calories — into her mouth. "Wizpeesher."

"What?"

"With Peter."

"Tch tch," said her mother. "Tch tch."

"What?"

"He's four years older than you are, Naomi, and not only that —"

"Ma, we're only going to look at funguses, for God's sake."

"Don't —"

"For gosh sake."

"You know I don't approve of some of Peter's . . . ideas. Why can't you see more of boys your own age?"

"Boys my own age are stupid."

"Forget boys then. What about Polly? She hasn't been around in weeks."

"Polly's busy with Crow."

"She has a pet crow?"

"It's her boyfriend's name, Ma."

"What — is he an Indian?"

"It's just a nickname."

"What about that other boy she was dating? What was his name — Cannonball?"

"Boom Boom, Ma, Boom Boom."

"I don't know how you expect me to keep track."

"You always want everything to stay the same." Naomi bit off the tip of the rabbit's ears.

"I've lived a little longer than you have. You can take my word — some things never change."

"You always say that. But you're wrong. Everything changes. It's a basic law of nature."

"Everything changes, and everything stays the same."

"If you want it to."

"What did you say?"

"Thou shalt eat roast chicken every Sunday."

"I wish you wouldn't talk with that chocolate in your mouth."

A person can go through her whole life with one set of rules, thought Naomi, with one set of ideas about how things are supposed to be. Her mother frowned down at the columns of figures. Everything neat, tidy, nothing unexpected ever happening — but how did it feel, to live such a tidy life? Everything must go so-o slow, the same routines day in and day out — but no. No, maybe everything speeded up, so that days and weeks and months and years slipped together, so that your whole life went by, so that one day you woke up and said, "I'm old, how did I ever come to be so old . . ."

A clanking, rattling, shuddering sound, a hundred tin cans

banging together, started up in the driveway. "Oh God, there's Peter."

"Don't say—"

"Oh gosh, there's Peter. I gotta go." Naomi pecked her mother on the cheek, then stopped. "Hey, Ma, I love you."

Surprised, her mother smiled and blushed faintly. "I love you, too."

"I know." Naomi kissed her again, and darted to the door. "I don't know if I'll be home for supper."

"You need a sweater! Remember to buckle your seat belt! And—"

"And I'll be good!"

"Naomi," said Peter, as she hopped into the VW.

"Peter."

The bug was orange, with one blue fender. Beneath Naomi's feet was an assorted collection of take-out coffee cups and empty sugar packets; the ashtray overflowed with brown-tipped pipe cleaners. Naomi had never been in the car before, and suddenly she felt shy.

"You smell like chocolate."

"Here." She broke off the rest of the bunny's ears and held them out to him.

"Umma umma," he said, around the hunk of candy, managing to look like a little boy and a man at the same time. He was wearing a sea-green sweater and jeans with one knee sticking out. "This was a good idea, Naomi. I'm glad we're doing this."

"Me, too," she said, her face growing warm. "Me, too." She picked at her wart.

"Where to?"

"Go up to the highway, then I'll tell you."

He backed the car out of the driveway, humming to himself. Naomi thought, He's in a better mood than I've seen him since Tess left. Now could that possibly, possibly, have anything to do with me?

They drove past the spook house, where the enormous beech tree was just beginning to leaf. The air in the car smelled of chocolate, and cherry tobacco, and, when she rolled down her window, fresh-cut grass. Naomi thought, I'm happy. I'm happy and I know it. This is a rare day. And it's only beginning.

Here I am.

"Hey, here's pretty Polly!" Peter suddenly stopped the car in front of the Quinn house.

Polly was sitting on her front steps, watching Cass do cartwheels on the lawn. When she saw the car she jumped up and turned two of them herself, one right after the other, right up to Peter's door. Her face in the window was flushed, her eyes startlingly blue. A strand of amber-colored hair was caught in her mouth.

"What does the world look like when you do that?" Peter asked her.

"Oooh, a kaleidoscope. Can't you do a cartwheel, Peter?"

"I used to be able to do a yoga headstand."

"I'll teach you," she teased, opening the car door, tugging on his arm. She was wearing jeans, and a white shirt sprigged with lavender flowers. "Right now, come on." Teasing, grinning. "Come on, Peter, out of that car."

"Not today. We're going on a picnic."

"Oh no, really?" She collapsed, pouting, against the car door. "I was just saying to Crow I'd give anything for one of us to be able to drive. On a day like this, I'm itching to get out into the real country!"

"Crow?" said Naomi, speaking for the first time. "I don't see Crow." There was only Cass, now hanging upside down from the spindly maple tree on the edge of the lawn, something gold and red glinting on her chest.

"He's out in the back with my mother, killing worms." Polly screwed up her face and stuck out her tongue. "A common passion," she explained to Peter.

"Why don't you come with us?"

Polly's eyes went at once to Naomi's face, to see if she would mind. But Naomi was staring down intently at the floor, at a sugar packet with a picture of Dwight D. Eisenhower on it.

"Well . . ." Polly looked back at Peter. "If you'll let me bring something. I just baked bread this morning. How about I bring a loaf?"

"It's a deal."

"I'll go get Crow."

Polly did another cartwheel and ran into the house. From the maple tree Cass gave them the evil eye. The upside-down evil eye. So did the gold bulldog with the red glass eye pinned to her shirt.

"This is turning into a party, huh, Naomi?"

"I guess so." She picked at her wart.

A minute later Polly came running out with a brown paper bag and Crow by the hand. They climbed into the back seat. "Crow, Peter, Peter, Crow — and of course you know Nome. Crow, yuck! What is this stuff all over my hand?"

"Wet flour. I told you I needed to wash my hands."

"Crow was killing worms. Oh, I told you that already. Where are we going? I don't care, don't tell me, I want to be surprised. I'll go anywhere, as long as it's out of this ticky-tacky neighborhood. Do you know how the people around here spend beautiful days like today? Vacuuming their lawns.

Strangling weeds. Dusting their flowers. I'm serious, the woman next door was out with her little pink dustcloth, dusting whatever that stuff is that crawls up the side of her house. Ivy, I guess."

"It's good for the leaves," said Naomi. "Ivy needs to be dusted." She turned in her seat. "Isn't that right, Crow?"

He looked up from chipping dried flour off his hand. "I don't know anything about ivy."

"Crow's just an old farmer, he only knows about his crops, right?" Polly patted his head. She made Naomi think of her little brother when he'd been cooped up in the house by bad weather; wound up tight, he'd hurl himself around, giddy and irritable, ready to laugh or cry at the drop of a hat. "Anyway, it might be good for the ivy but it can't be good for the people. They just fritter away their lives, fussing and keeping up with the neighbors."

"And then they go to the shopping centers to try and fill up their empty lives by buying things, trying to find some satisfaction in possessions." Peter nodded.

"Exactly!" Polly bounced on her seat. "Exactly, Peter. Hey, doesn't a super-luxury car like this have a radio?"

"No," said Naomi, finally getting a word in.

"Oh yes it does — look." Polly leaned over, one hand on Peter's shoulder, and turned an imaginary radio dial. She made a static-y noise in her throat and then began to sing:

> *This morning sun*
> *Has me all undone,*
> *Makin' rainbows on my wall,*
> *And the birds begin to call . . .*

To Naomi's astonishment — she had never heard him sing before — Peter joined in.

Now out of bed,
Raise your sleepy head.
Dress yourself in sunshine,
'Cause this day is yours and mi-ine!

Naomi didn't know the words; neither did Crow, or else he was too shy to sing. Naomi had a vague memory of him throwing up once, while singing. Sitting with her hands between her knees, which suddenly looked fat, she stared down at Dwight D. Eisenhower. "Our 34th President," she read, as Peter and Polly sang,

'Cause today is yours and mi-ine!

"Do you know any Judy Collins, Polly?"

"Which album?"

Half turning, Naomi looked at Crow. He gave the distinct impression this picnic wasn't his idea at all.

"Naomi, where are we going? I forgot what you said," laughed Peter.

Polly, pretty Polly, come, go along with me,
Polly, pretty Polly, come, go along with me,
Before we get married . . .

Polly knew every song Peter started. He doesn't sing well at all, thought Naomi. He should confine it to the shower. But that doesn't seem to bother him. Look at him laughing. Did he used to sing to Tess? He's never sung to me.

Faintly, deep inside, Naomi began to hear a once-familiar sound. *Ding ding!* It made her sit up straighter, on guard. *Ding ding!*

Before we get married, some pleasure to see-e-e . . .

Polly reached over and rubbed Peter's fuzzy head, something Naomi had been wanting to do since the first day she met him.

Peter turned up onto the highway. They passed the Sunshine Motel, which advertised, "Children 16 and Under FREE!!!"

Polly said, "When he was sixteen Boom Boom took a girl in there and demanded a free room. Can you believe it?"

Out of the corner of her eye, Naomi caught Crow's wince.

"Turn here," she commanded Peter. They left the highway, gray ribbon knotted with storefronts and signs, and were among the trees and fields and fancy houses. A little farther on, "Here, pull over here," she told him.

Jumping out of the car, Polly pulled Naomi aside. "You don't mind, do you? Our coming along?"

"Now she asks me."

"No, really, do you? Because we can always wander off by ourselves now." Polly jiggled from one foot to the other.

"We only came to look at funguses, it's no big deal."

"So you say."

"Don't look at me like that. You're worse than my mother."

"I really did have to get out. I was being eaten up with claustrophobia. Everything was getting on my nerves." She stopped. "I don't know — spring always makes me restless. Maybe it's my father in me."

It occurred to Naomi that Polly was trying to make her feel sorry for her, and so forgive her for barging in on the picnic. But she decided that was an unkind thought. "It's okay," she said heavily, realizing how accustomed she was to giving way to Polly.

Polly gave her a quick hug, then ran on ahead, crying, when she saw the NO TRESPASSING signs, "Do you think we'll get shot at?"

A few weeks ago the earth was still so bare and brown that each green shoot was precious; now new life was everywhere. The tips of the tree branches had exploded into fireworks of yellow, red, and pale green flowers.

"Like earrings," Polly said, breaking off a cluster of yellow blooms from a sassafras tree and dangling it from her ear. "Or a mustache." She held a green winged key under Crow's nose.

"Those are two seeds," Naomi told her. "See how they're joined together?"

"It looks like two fish kissing," said Polly, smiling and holding it up for them to see. Naomi looked at Peter, expecting him to roll his eyes at Polly's silliness, but he was smiling, too.

"Oh, look what I found!" Polly fell to her knees beside a handful of stars tossed in the grass.

"The bloodroot," said Naomi.

Polly bent her face to them, her long red-gold hair mingling with their white and yellow shine. Crow looked down at her as if she were a wildflower herself.

This is where Danny kissed me that day. Where he said, "Your eyes have little gold crinkles, like this." Where I promised to bring him back, to see these very flowers . . .

"Nome, is this *it?*" Polly's voice came sailing back from far ahead. It was impossible to keep up with her. "This is *it*, isn't it, Nome?"

There she stood beside the shipwrecked car. For Naomi it was like a bad dream made real.

"That's it, all right." She didn't break her stride. "I wouldn't stand there if I were you — the mosquitoes have hatched in that water."

She hurried on, walking fast so the pain wouldn't have a

chance to catch hold, the way she swallowed waffles quickly so the calories wouldn't stick. Her feet squished in the mud, a strand of spider silk strung across the path broke on her cheek — and suddenly she realized she didn't hear any voices, or any footsteps but her own. She turned; the path behind her was empty. Naomi sank down onto a fallen tree.

After what seemed a very long time — she saw a rabbit, velvet ears quivering, but she wouldn't tell them about it — they came along. The path was overgrown here, and barely wide enough for Peter and Polly to walk side by side, arms nearly touching. Peter gestured and talked while Polly, her head to one side and wearing a small smile, listened. Crow, his black hair in his eyes, straggled along behind, tripping over rocks and roots and, it seemed, his own two feet.

"I was just telling Polly what a great example of symbiosis the lichen is. The union of two individuals: the alga and the fungus. Each could make it on its own, but they'd have a much rougher time. The relationship used to be parasitic — the fungus just fed off the alga — but over millions of years of evolution they've developed this more mutual relationship. They both gain, so it's a more permanent association."

"Symbiosis," repeated Polly, her head to one side.

"The fungus derives nourishment, and the alga derives protection. Let me tell you about the man-of-war jellyfish."

"Creepy," said Polly.

"Not only creepy — incredibly poisonous. Lethal, in fact. There's a little blue-and-gray fish, though, that swims in and out among its tentacles with impunity."

"Nomeus," called Naomi, but Polly and Peter had already started to walk on, and neither turned around.

Naomi wheeled on Crow and said furiously, "You know, I'm the one who knows my way around these woods —

they've never even been here before! Why am I following them?"

Crow's eyebrows made a movement that reminded her of the lids of two dark boxes suddenly flipped open. "I didn't even want to come," he said apologetically. "I've been working all vacation and I meant to spend the day in my garden."

"It's not your fault. I didn't mean it was your fault."

Crow pushed his hair out of his eyes and unhooked his sweater from the branch it had caught on. Peter and Polly were far ahead, and Naomi and Crow followed in silence. Naomi considered asking him if he remembered that time in seventh grade when they danced together, but decided they both felt rotten enough without being reminded of seventh grade. She considered saying, "If you don't stand up to her once in a while, she'll never respect you — believe me, I know"; but she decided she had better mind her own business. So they trudged along without speaking, Polly's laughter and the low rumble of Peter's voice carrying back to them across the warm, moist air.

When Naomi and Crow caught up to them, they were standing in a small clearing, soft grass ringed with young birches and sumac. Sunlight poured down on them, edging Polly's hair with a halo. They looked as if they were posing for one of those photo greeting cards that show beautiful people in a beautiful setting.

"Let's have our picnic here — it's the perfect spot!" Polly's eyes, violet-blue now, were dancing. Naomi thought wistfully of how she'd meant to lead Peter to this very spot. Alone. "Come on now, sit down, the grass is lovely, I'll cut my bread."

Polly took out her loaf, a shining golden braid, and cut thick slices. Naomi set out her few apples and bruised pears.

Peter leaned against one of the birch trees, his hair looking furrier than ever against its paper-white bark, and Crow just about sat on top of Polly, anchoring her.

"*Déjeuner sur l'herbe!*" said Polly, meaning God knows what. "And now, my surprise!" She snatched up the brown paper bag lying in the grass and pulled out a bottle. "*Vin!*"

"Wine?"

"How'd you ever manage that?"

She waved the big bottle in the air. "Boom Boom bought it once, for a picnic we never went on. He picked it out — he said it would be excellent."

Crow took the bottle from her and looked at it.

"This is crap," he said.

Polly stared at him. "Since when are you an authority on wine?"

"This isn't any better than grape Kool-Aid."

Polly took it back. "Then you don't want any, I guess," she said, with a look Naomi had seen somewhere before. "Peter, would you open this, please?" She held out the bottle and corkscrew.

"Look, I don't want to get arrested for corrupting the morals of minors, you know."

"We're all adults. I thought."

Crow seemed to shrink around his edges.

"Well, I'll make you all walk a straight line before I let you back in my car." *Pop!* Polly handed him three paper cups, and passed them out as he filled them. "Here, Crow," he said, reaching for a fourth. "You have to have some, too, so we can have a toast. To . . . to what? I'm never any good at making toasts."

"To symbiosis." Polly touched her cup to his.

The wine was sweet and bubbly and Naomi felt it at once,

like tiny fingers drumming inside her head. In her excitement that morning, she hadn't eaten any breakfast. She wasn't much of a drinker; she hadn't really had anything to drink since that pajama party where she'd tried beer, wine, and peppermint schnapps, all at once, all for the first time, and been sick for three days.

"Not bad."

"Thank you, Peter. Here, have some homemade bread." Polly handed around crumbly slices of her shining loaf. She held one out to Crow, and Naomi saw him touch the back of her hand.

"No, not bad at all," said Peter. "And this bread—this is some delicious bread. You could get yourself elected the first woman President, Polly, if you went around handing out slices of this bread."

"I'll give you my recipe. Here, have another piece. Have some more wine." Polly, the hostess, touched up each one's cup.

"We didn't expect to wind up like this, did we, Naomi?" Peter leaned back against the birch tree and smiled at her.

"No, we sure didn't."

A party. The day I brought Danny here, he said, "This'd be a great place for a party," and I knew I'd never forgive him. A party in these solemn woods—how could he even think of it? Now here I am. Drinking wine with Peter. Drinking with Peter! In all the times she'd been upstairs, Naomi and he had never done anything more mind-expanding than Twinkies. Naomi took a large gulp of the sweet wine.

"This is wonderful, absolutely wonderful." Polly leaned back on her elbows, her hair a red-gold pool in the grass. They all looked at her as if she were the centerpiece, the bouquet of roses in the center of their table. "It was pretty selfish of you to keep this place a secret so long, Naomi."

Naomi didn't answer.

"This is just what I needed! I was getting to feel so cooped up, like a person in one of those movies where the walls keep getting closer and closer together."

"It's the suburbs," said Peter, helping himself to more wine. "There aren't any open places left. Every square inch is fenced off, plastered with these 'No Trespassing' signs. Of course you realize this very moment we're all breaking the law, just by sitting here enjoying the grass and the trees."

"We're lucky they're here at all! We're lucky they weren't wiped out, the way that potato farm was so they could build that blight on the face of this earth, Laughing Brooks." Polly shook her head, poured herself more wine.

"The only natural places left for you kids to go are the parks, which are about as natural as a baloney sandwich on white bread, and the beaches, which are polluted. No wonder you feel closed in. I don't blame Naomi for keeping this place secret. Everybody needs a place where they can go and feel alone. When I was growing up there was a little patch of woods near my house. In spring I'd catch sunnies in the stream there. I'd watch them swim around in my pail for a while, and then I'd let them go. There were water spiders, and frogs — it was where I first really got interested in biology. Then they sold it, brought in a bulldozer, and started to clear it for a shopping center. One night I snuck out of the house with my father's hacksaw and sawed off the bulldozer's gear shaft."

"What happened?" gasped Polly, sitting up.

"They got another bulldozer."

"Aah." She sank back down, shaking her head tragically.

Peter shook his head. Naomi shook her head, and felt something rattle. She poured herself more wine.

"Beauty is where you find it," she heard herself say.

"Nome is so adaptable. Next she'll be saying, 'If you can't say something nice, don't say anything at all' What Peter says is true. The suburbs are a waste."

"You're always putting down Laughing Brooks." Naomi took another gulp of wine. Things were happening inside her; everything seemed to be speeding up. "But I don't see what's so bad about it. I think it's nice there. I think it's nice people care so much about their houses and their lawns, and work so hard for their kids. You could find worse ways to live your life."

"Like being locked up in jail, you mean?"

"I'm serious!" Why am I getting so angry? Why does this suddenly seem so important? Naomi had no idea, especially since if she and Peter were alone, she'd probably be agreeing with him. But something about the sight of Peter and Polly sitting there so smug and sure of themselves, nodding over their wine and ripping other people's lives to shreds — it made her angry. Very. "You can have your opinions, but remember that's all they are."

"Still, Nome," said Peter, using Polly's nickname for the first time, "still, how many adults do you know who are happy? Or not even happy — just satisfied? Don't you find most of them feel cheated somehow?"

"Well, I don't know. I never asked them that."

"You don't have to ask, you can just see it," Polly said impatiently.

"Maybe *you* can see it —"

"Anyway," said Peter, "the suburbs are doomed. So is the nuclear family. Statistics speak the facts."

"A lot of people would argue with those 'facts,'" Naomi said carefully, concentrating so she'd get every word right.

"Do you have to be so defensive?" Polly tossed back her hair.

"Naomi's going to college," Peter told Polly.

"She is? I didn't even know she was thinking about it."

"She hasn't decided yet," said Naomi loudly. "And I'm not being defensive." Her head felt wobbly, as if it were balanced on a pivot. For a moment she imagined herself as one of those little dolls in the rear windows of cars, smiling blankly and nodding constantly. "Or maybe I am. So what. The easiest thing in the world is to criticize. And to talk and sound smart and say all those things. That's easy, but what really counts is feelings." Naomi went to take another sip of wine and was amazed to find her cup empty.

"Well, anyway," yawned Polly, the conversation obviously beginning to bore her. "Anyway, I was feeling cooped up and now I don't. Peter, would you like some more bread?"

"Umma." Naomi watched him take another thick slice. *Ding ding!*

"Here, Peter, have one of my apples. Have one of my pears. I know, have some jelly beans."

"Jelly beans!" cried Polly, reaching over and taking the bag. "You brought jelly beans?"

"Yes, I brought belly jeans. Jelly beans. They're not all that rare, you know."

"Look at all this stuff!" Polly pulled out a yellow marshmallow chicken. "You must've been a good girl for the Easter Bunny to bring you all this stuff." She took a jelly bean and held it out to Crow.

"I don't like jelly beans."

"What! I never in my life met anyone who didn't like

jelly beans." Polly swallowed it herself. "But then, Crow has strange tastes. He doesn't like popcorn, either."

Naomi saw his brows make that movement again, the lids of ebony boxes flying open. It made him look so forlorn she had the impulse to say, "I hate popcorn, too" — even though she loved it. Polly poured out the rest of the wine, then lay back, her head on Crow's knee, and began to play with his fingers. It flashed through Naomi's speeded-up brain that flirting with Crow was a way of flirting with Peter.

"So, Polly, what do you plan to do when you bust out of Laughing Brooks?" asked Peter.

"Let's see. Live in Paris, in an apartment overlooking a garden, and have breakfast brought to me in bed each morning, on a tray with a fresh gardenia." She dropped Crow's fingers and waved a willowy arm in the air. "Maybe write best-sellers and be photographed going to exclusive parties with a man in a black eye patch."

Peter smiled; Polly looked beautiful, with her eyes closed and a small yellow leaf tangled in her hair. *Ding ding!* Naomi wished they had never come on this picnic, that she and Peter had stayed up in his apartment, their sanctuary, drinking cream soda and reading about the wonders of the water world.

"Wonders of the water world," she said aloud, but no one noticed.

"I'd also like to discover a new star. And learn how to sky dive. And meet Jane Fonda." Crow sat with his head a little to one side, looking at her. He was waiting — Naomi could tell with the ESP she seemed to have acquired, along with the wobbling head and speeded-up brain — waiting for Polly to mention him in her plans for the future. Of course she wouldn't. Naomi knew that, too. Poor Crow. Naomi saw there was trouble ahead for him.

Ding ding ding! Peter smiled, Polly talked, Crow waited. Did Crow hear alarms like this, too?

"How about living in a castle on a cliff above the Rhine, with a one-armed servant named Lothar?"

Naomi finished her wine and wished there was more. Crow began to shred his paper cup. For a moment his features seemed to dissolve and reshape themselves as Danny's. Or was it herself she saw? He and I look like brother and sister. Naomi shook her wobbly head. Some things never change, my mother says. Naomi looked at Crow looking at Polly and felt him asking her, *Do you want me? Please look at me and want me.*

Polly twirled a strand of hair around her finger and laughed. Peter laughed, too, and Naomi realized she had missed a joke. DING DING DING. She laughed, too late. Crow sat solemn, shredding his cup to nothing. If Polly and Peter got up and walked away into the woods together this very minute, Crow would go on sitting there, ripping up his cup. He was no good at games. No good at playing Who Likes Who? Who likes who *more?*

If no one loves you, you don't exist. That was a law of nature so basic they didn't even bother to mention it in the biology books.

Polly sat up, tossing her hair.

"I hope there really is such a thing as reincarnation, so you'll get to live all those lives," said Peter. Polly reached over and rubbed his downy head.

DING DING DING! Naomi tried to think of something funny or incredibly profound to say. All that came into her head was, Why did I bring them here? These woods were ruined for her now; she didn't see how she'd ever feel alone or peaceful here again.

Now Polly was talking about going up to Peter's and showing him how to make bread. Naomi searched frantically for something to say. She couldn't just yell, "Look at me — look at Naomi Denning!"

"Swedish limpa, you'd like that bread, Peter. It has just the slightest tang of —"

"I have a wart!" Naomi burst out, so loudly and so suddenly that Polly paused in midsentence, openmouthed.

"You what?"

"I have a wart. See? Right here on my thumb. It just appeared one day. Popped up like a mushroom. Want to see?" Naomi jumped up and went around showing each of them.

"That's very interesting, Nome," said Polly, grinning. Looking at Peter, she put a finger to her temple and made a little circle. "Vino madness," she stage-whispered.

"I read somewhere that they can remove warts by hypnosis," said Crow, and they all turned to look at him. This was the longest sentence they'd heard him utter all day.

"That's ridiculous," said Peter. "Warts are caused by a virus. There's no way hypnotism could affect them."

"You have to go out and kiss a frog at midnight," said Polly, holding Naomi's thumb up before her. "Oooh, it's really hideous, Nome."

"There have been documented cases," insisted Crow. "I read it."

"You have no idea how complicated a virus is. I don't know much about it myself, but I know the body has to go through a very, very complex process in order to expel one. Believe me, no one waving a shiny object before your face and saying, 'You are getting sleepy,' is going to have a chance against a virus."

"My mother had a wart removed," said Polly. "First they have to freeze it, then —"

Naomi snatched her thumb back from Polly so suddenly that Polly toppled over. "It's my wart!" she cried. "Who said I wanted it frozen? Who said I wanted it hypnotized? It's my wart and I'm keeping it!"

"All right, all right, calm down," said Polly. "What's wrong? Are you drunk, Nome?"

"And don't call me Nome, either. Why do you always call me that? No one else does."

"I like calling you that." Polly smiled. "Nome and Crow, my two best friends."

"I hate the sound of it. Nome. Gnome. It makes me sound as if I'm some troll or something, some ugly, warty —" She stopped, clutching her thumb.

"I've been calling you that for seven years," Polly said slowly, still sitting where Naomi had toppled her. "You never seemed to mind before."

"Well, I mind now."

"All right." Polly sat up, dusting off her hands. "I'll try to remember."

"And it's my wart, and nobody's going to hypnotize it or say it's hideous or anything else, understand?" Looking at their faces, Naomi realized she was yelling. "Understand?" she repeated, in what she hoped was a more normal voice.

Polly sat very still. "I don't think you should drink wine, No— Naomi."

"And I think you should shut up."

Polly blinked. "What did you say?"

Peter scrambled up, scattering bread and jelly beans. "I think it's time to go."

Polly got slowly to her feet. She touched Naomi's arm. "Are you so angry at me?" she asked softly. "I didn't know."

"Time to go," boomed Peter, fake-hearty.

"I guess it is," said Polly, as Naomi, eyes cast down, found no words.

They rode all the way home without speaking. Once she sank into the front seat, Naomi was suddenly so sleepy she could barely keep her head up. Through half-closed eyes she saw Dwight D. Eisenhower smiling up at her. He had big ears. She kept burping and tasting jelly beans. She'd never eat them again.

Peter pulled up in front of Polly's house. Crow mumbled something.

"Goodbye," said Polly.

"Goodbye." The word seemed to hang in the air, like a note struck on a tuning fork.

In the Dennings' driveway Peter turned in his seat and looked at Naomi. She waited for him to say, "Wow, you really are a baby." He said, "How do you feel?"

"My head hurts."

"I shouldn't have let you drink that wine."

"It was my fault. I'm not used to it. And I had an empty stomach. For once in my life." She must have still been a little high because she heard herself add, "I got jealous of Polly."

"How?"

Though sure her mother was watching them from behind the dining-room curtains, and though almost too logy to talk, she went on, "How? Every way. She's so pretty, and funny, and smart. I've always been jealous of her, I guess."

"That's a strange basis for a friendship that's lasted all these years."

"We're symbiotic. We feed off each other."

"All friends do that. And lovers. It's only bad when one person begins to gobble up too much of the other."

To her horror, Naomi burped right out loud. "Oh God," she said, and moved to get out.

"Wait." Peter put a hand on her arm. "You shouldn't be jealous of her." Naomi looked at him. He picked off a burdock stuck to her sleeve. "You shouldn't be jealous," he repeated gently. "There's something you have, something inside you, that shines out — I see it all the time. That was a beautiful place you took us to. It was wonderful of you to share it. And you were right, what you said about feelings."

He remembers what I said. Oh God, what did I say?

"What you said about talk being cheap, but real feelings, like you have . . ."

Yes? Real feelings like I have? Yes?

He shook his head, rubbed his bald knee. "I should never have let you drink all that wine. I feel bad about it. I know — how about coming up and having a cup of tea before you go in?" He plucked off another burdock. "Chamomile. That's supposed to be soothing."

His hand still on her arm. That hair like fox fur. He doesn't think I'm an idiot. We can go right back to how things were. He's still touching me. Naomi leaned toward him; she opened her lips to say, "There is nothing that would make me happier than to share a cup of chamomile tea with you."

A tap on her window. In slow motion, moving through water, Naomi turned her head.

Tess was standing there. Smiling, and holding a suitcase.

"She had too much of that cr— that wine," Crow said. "You shouldn't let it bother you, her saying shut up."

"She would've said a lot more, if Peter hadn't herded us all into his car."

"A lot more?"

"She was really mad at me, didn't you notice?" Polly peered up into the beech tree's branches. "Poor Nome, she probably thought I was after Peter or something. That's a joke. Him and his lectures on fungus. She can have him."

Crow leaned against the tree. "You look different when you say things like that. Your face changes."

"Please don't start. How come you suddenly have so much to say? You hardly said one word all afternoon, and now you're going to start making everything so serious." She tore a just-opened leaf from the tree. "It's a problem with you, Crow."

"But this *is* serious, Polly. Naomi's your best friend, and I can tell you're shook up—"

"Oh, will you leave me alone? I'm going home."

"Don't go away mad. We've never gone away from each other mad."

Polly looked at him, and the clenched place inside her loosened. "Okay. I just want to go home."

"Okay. I'll see you tomorrow. In school. Whoopee."

"Yeah."

She walked to the corner, knowing he stood watching her out of sight, the way he always did, but she didn't turn. She walked home through the gathering dusk, past the Denning house; there was a candle burning in Peter's window, and she wondered if Naomi was up there. By the time she got home she had decided to call Naomi and have an Instant Replay.

But Mrs. Denning told her, "Naomi doesn't feel well. She's gone to bed."

Chapter Twenty-five

Polly stood in the hall outside Personality, staring at the floor. The custodians had waxed it over vacation, and she could almost see herself in it. Why did they bother? In two days it would look exactly like it did before.

She leaned against a cold locker. Inside, in Personality, they were playing one of Mr. Haight's games: Metamorphoses. It was her turn to be "it" and guess. Stupid game. And Crow. Sitting across the circle of desks, twirling a small bunch of violets. Another present. Everything she'd said to him yesterday had just rolled off his back. She should call him Duck, not Crow.

The first day back from vacation. The prom was a month away. Across the hall the committee had hung its first posters. A cartoon balloon issued from the mouth of a baseball player, his mitt held up: "The Prom — Catch It!" Polly felt terrible. She had a pimple in the corner of her mouth. Polly never got pimples. All last night she'd wondered what would happen when she saw Naomi today, but Naomi had solved that problem: she was absent.

Polly considered walking down the hall and out the door. She could say she suddenly felt sick, and had to go. She was in no mood to play games, no mood for anything but being left alone. She took a step toward the exit.

"Hey, gal, you ready for this?" Boom Boom stuck his head out the classroom door. His tangled, vanilla-fudge hair looked blonder than ever against his honey-tan skin.

"'Gal'? You're really crazy, you know that? You really should get help. Yes, I'm ready." Chin in the air, Polly breezed past him. Might as well get this over with. She took her seat.

"If this person were a flower," she asked, "what kind of flower would he or she be?"

"Day lily."

"Rosebud," said Crow.

"Venus flytrap," drawled Boom Boom, and everyone laughed. He twirled the cowboy hat Mr. Haight wouldn't let him wear in class.

"That's not a flower," objected Polly.

"You're right. Make it a cactus flower."

Again they all laughed, all except Crow, and Polly shifted in her seat. "Well, what kind of animal?"

"Fish," said Marcia Melon, wrinkling her little nose and swaying her big earrings.

"Hummingbird," said Crow.

"A chameleon." Boom Boom broke the class up again. He put on his hat, grinning.

"Mr. Bottzemeyer, remove your headgear and make some pretense of manners, if you would," said Mr. Haight.

"A chameleon?" repeated Polly. "A fish, a hummingbird, and a chameleon? This must be one weird person. What kind of book?"

"Poetry," from Crow.

"Mystery," said Boom Boom.

"Sandwich?"

"Dry toast." Boom Boom got his laugh on cue. Polly felt the back of her throat get tight. What was going on? Crow was looking at Boom Boom as if he might leap up and kick him in the stomach. Mr. Haight raised a hand.

"Mr. Bottzemeyer, if you cannot control your wit, and I use that term loosely, I may have to ask you to remove yourself from the premises."

Boom Boom regarded his cowboy hat somberly, but the

corners of his mouth twitched with repressed laughter. Polly took a deep breath and went on. "How about climate?"

"Very changeable."

"Season?"

"Spring." Crow twirled the violets.

"Summer."

"Winter."

"Fall."

"Now wait a minute. How can this person be every season?"

"Polly, the bell is about to ring," said Mr. Haight. "Why don't you take a guess?"

"I have no idea."

"How about body of water?" said Boom Boom in a helpful, repentant tone. "You still haven't asked body of water."

"Okay. If this person were a body of water, what kind would she or he be?"

"An icicle," said Boom Boom, without missing a beat, and the bell rang.

"It was you, silly," tittered Marcia Melon, earrings brushing her shoulders. "Didn't you know it was you?" she asked, as people shuffled out.

"Mr. Bottzemeyer, if you will." Mr. Haight crooked a finger. Polly grabbed up her books and pushed through the knot of people filing out. She heard Mr. Haight call her name, but didn't stop. She hurried down the hall and out the first door, cutting across the parking lot toward the school's other wing.

"Polly! Polly, wait!" Crow came running up to her, grabbed her elbow. "Why didn't you wait for me?" He pushed the hair out of his eyes.

"I wasn't thinking of you" She retrieved her elbow without breaking her stride

"Don't let him hurt you."

"Hurt? Ha, don't make me laugh. That'll be the day, when he hurts me."

"It's because you're going out with me now He's jealous."

"You think I need you to tell me that?"

"He's just jealous."

Polly stopped in her tracks and looked at him. "Why do you keep saying that?"

"Because it's true."

"No, that's not why. You like the sound of it, that's why. You like the idea of someone being jealous of you. It's a big thrill. It makes you feel like you own me."

"Huh?"

"Well, forget that, Crow, because you don't. And you can stop trying to stick up for me all the time, too. First with Naomi, now with Boom Boom. I don't need anyone to defend me, you know. I do fine on my own. I have for a long time now."

Crow just looked at her. "I never thought I owned you."

"Well, don't start thinking it, okay? I have to go. I can't be late for Lee's class."

"You're coming to the garden this afternoon?"

"I don't know. I have stuff to do."

"You haven't been there in a week. Wait'll you see the peas."

"Look, it's your garden, Crow. What do you need me there for? I said I don't know. If I come, I come — don't wait for me." She yanked open the heavy glass door and let it swing to behind her, leaving Crow standing there alone on the step, still holding the drooping violets.

Chapter Twenty-six

She cut her last two classes and went walking, along the highway, in and out of the other neighborhoods that bordered her own. She felt both inside and out the way her elbow or her knee used to when her mother whipped off a Band-Aid. She was afraid if she saw Boom Boom she might throw something at his head. Or possibly even cry. She did cry, right in Lee's chemistry lab, three tears splashing onto the Bunsen burner, making it sputter, before she caught herself. It wasn't any good telling herself that Boom would sell his own grandmother for a laugh, or that the class laughed at his jokes as automatically as they scratched their itches. She still hurt.

Hurt. Today she'd hurt Crow for the first time, on purpose. It was there in the air between them, glinting like the flash of a knife, or the swift downsweep of a bird's wing. And she didn't take it back. She let the door swing to in his face.

Boom Boom → Polly → Crow. You could diagram the hurt being passed along, as neatly as Catherine had her students diagram sentences, as accurately as any equation in chemistry. But in the end the sentence made no sense. And in the end there was still the hurt, the end product of fission or fusion or whatever it was, a charged mass floating free in the air. What would Crow do with it? Go home and punch a wall? Probably he would work in his garden, tending the small green things until he felt calmer; he would never strike back at her, that was the thing. He needed her too much. It was knowing that that had made her want to hurt him today. It was so easy to hurt Crow — he stood there like a target — he let her roll up all Boom Boom's cruelty into a ball and hurl it right in his face.

There was a demon inside her. Touching her pimple gingerly, for it had begun to swell, Polly remembered Mrs. Mulehead. When she was small, and did anything wrong, she always blamed it on Mrs. Mulehead. When the pickles on the shelf next to the forbidden cookies suddenly smashed to the floor, it was that bad old Mrs. Mulehead who did it, not Polly.

Mrs. Mulehead — or the demon — no, it was you. No one else but you.

The pimple felt as if it were swelling. It made her think of Naomi and her wart. Naomi yelling at her — wine or no wine, that had never happened before. Why had Naomi stayed home today? As she walked up her driveway Polly thought she felt something brush her head and she looked up, Chicken Little, expecting to see the sky falling.

Mrs. Quinn was out in the back painting the garage. The junior high had closed early because of bomb threats. Could Polly imagine that? Of course there was no bomb, and of course now it would be happening every other day. Wearing one of Polly's old shirts, a scarf over her hair, Mrs. Quinn slapped her brush back and forth and composed a letter to the local newspaper out loud. Suddenly she stopped.

"Well, don't you look like an old mope. What's the matter?"

"Nothing."

"Go change your clothes and come out and help me. A little physical exercise will do you good."

"I don't —"

"Go on, go on!"

A few minutes later they were standing side by side, the sun on their shoulders, each holding a coffee can of white paint, spattering the grass with little milky dots.

"You're right. I do feel better."

"There's nothing like physical labor to chase away those broodies." Her mother took a step back and surveyed her work. Putting down her brush and can, she lit a cigarette. "What could be more satisfying than looking on something you've made? Of course, a mother gets that pleasure every day. But I've often thought I missed my calling. I should have been a carpenter. Or a construction worker."

"Your students would flip to hear that."

"Wouldn't they? I was born thirty years too soon. Do you know what my most cherished fantasy was, once upon a time?"

"No, what?"

"To be a truck driver. You laugh! But I saw myself quite clearly, barreling down some highway in the middle of the night, no company but my radio and that long strip of white line stretching out before me." Mrs. Quinn drew on her cigarette, narrowed her eyes. "I'd pull into some city I'd never seen before, find the truckers' favorite greasy spoon, order my coffee black and my eggs over easy, double order of home fries—"

"You'd play Johnny Cash on the jukebox."

"Right! And pick my teeth with a matchbook cover." Mrs. Quinn sighed. "Of course there were no such things as lady truck drivers in those days, which is probably the reason I married your father. I suppose every life has to have its one great romantic gesture."

Polly went on painting.

"I'm sorry. I shouldn't malign your father like that."

"That's okay."

"If I were a better mother I'd say only good things about him. I'd give you a positive male image."

"It's okay, Mom. Everybody has to let off steam once in a while."

"Even me. You're right." Catherine ground out her cigarette. "You understand I'm not complaining. I love my house, this yard . . ."

"I know."

"Along with my two daughters, this is what I have wrought. I wouldn't trade it for all the tea in China. Still . . ." She paused, a wrinkle of smile around her eyes. "Still, I warn you, don't be surprised if the day Cass leaves home you catch sight of your mother careening by in a tractor trailer." She gave Polly a little poke, picked up her coffee can.

Polly watched her slap on the broad white strokes, leaving no trace of the old, cracked paint. She thought of telling her mother what had happened in Personality, but before she could decide to, her mother asked, in her crisp, spelling-bee voice, "What's become of that Jonathon Stephens? I thought you'd be working in his garden this afternoon."

"I haven't been there in a while." The back of Polly's throat closed. "He was working at Wally's all vacation."

"Industrious."

"Umm."

"Serious."

"Umm."

"About you." Mrs. Quinn carefully trimmed an edge, the center of her brow creased in a frown Polly knew well. "What about you?"

The words just squeezed out: "I don't know."

"I'm sorry if I'm prying, Polly, but I have to admit I'm curious. And—a little concerned." She regarded her work, chewed her lower lip. "It's not like you to see so much of one boy, especially one who seems quite capable of falling madly in love, if you don't mind my saying so. I can imagine him asking you to elope, or something equally melodramatic, and the more I see you getting involved — well." The lines in Mrs. Quinn's forehead knotted, gathered like a fist. "I just hate the thought of you getting hurt."

I already am! Polly wanted to cry. Can't you see I already am? You can't live without getting hurt — you of all people should know. Hearts can't be locked away for safekeeping. Polly watched her mother spread the paint in shining white strokes, hiding the old paint, covering the wound with clean white gauze.

For once can't we just throw ourselves into each other's arms and cry?

But Catherine would fold her arms across her chest and say, "Self-pity never got anyone anywhere." Wouldn't she? And if she did, how could I stand it?

"You don't have to worry about me, Mom. I'm doing okay."

"Good. I know you are, Polly."

They went on painting, side by side, and soon the whole back of the garage was gleaming and white, not a crack or speck of dirt showing.

That night Crow called Polly, something he rarely did. He wasn't good at talking over the phone.

"I was thinking," he said. "What you said about Boom Boom and Naomi, how you don't need me to stick up for you? You're right, and I'll try not to do it anymore. But I was thinking something else, too. Did you notice the only time we have arguments they're about other people? It makes me wish we could just go and live in our tree house alone. Just the two of us, away from everything."

❦ 171 ❧

"But that's not how it is," said Polly. "That's not the way it is."

This is how it is, Naomi told herself, lying in bed and staring at her ceiling, their floor. This is how it is: He loves Tess. He has never stopped loving her, not for one minute. Now she's come back to him.

And you are on your own. You have been, all along, whether you knew it or not.

Chapter Twenty-seven

"Hey, old man, git yerself a drink here."

"Thank ya kindly, Ma. Genuine one hunnert percent lemonade! Well, bless my boots!"

Crow took the glass from Polly and drank it down in one swallow, wiped his mouth with the back of his hand. "Better 'n moonshine," he said, leaning on his hoe. His shirt was dark under the arms and down the back, just the way it was that first day, out in Wally's parking lot. "This here garden's becomin' a right purty sight, eh, Ma?"

"A regular feast for the eyes, Pa."

"It'll be a feast fer yer belly, 'fore too long."

Crow's wish to "put down roots for real" had come true. Row on row of growing things misted the raw earth green. On the back steps, like infants in their cradles, tomato and cucumber seedlings grew in flats. Fat bumblebees drowsed among the last of the pea blossoms. The pods were forming and the plants were tall, clinging to the fence Crow had made. Bits of his father's old undershirt fluttered in the breeze. They were meant to scare away birds but there was a robin, fat and undaunted, pecking away in a carefully weeded row. Leaning on his hoe, Crow was proud of his garden, so proud he was embarrassed, like a new father.

"Reckon I'll git to the lower forty tomorrow, Ma."

"You'd best, Pa." Polly hadn't been here for two weeks. Now that she knew what it reminded her of, this house made her uneasy. That, and Crow, his eyes constantly asking her, *It's okay, isn't it? We're okay?* "I'll go get some more lemonade."

In the kitchen the table was laid just the way it always was: the half-drunk cup of coffee, leaving a circle on the open newspaper, the box of junk pastry that seemed, this warm day, to be sweating. Polly got the pitcher and went back out quickly; the sight of that table, its tablecloth with its two worn circles, was more than she could take today.

"Ma, yer a good woman. Worth every penny of the two bucks I laid out fer that there marriage license." Crow drank down another glass of lemonade, brushed his hair out of his eyes, and then, in that way of his, suddenly became all seriousness. Setting his glass on the rusty metal chair, he slipped an arm around her waist and said, "You know, when I play around like that, well . . . Just now when you went inside and I was standing here looking at the garden, I imagined what it'd be like — not that we'd ever live in a crummy place like this, but . . . what it'd be like if we were really, you know, really married. I do that sometimes, when you're sitting there in the chair and I'm working, and sometimes even when you're not here. . . . Polly."

And he kissed her, though his hands were caked with earth and though the kids playing next door shrieked through the fence and though, if he'd opened his eyes, he'd have seen the trapped look in hers.

That night as she sat in her room supposedly studying for a history test but really staring at the ceiling and her toes and getting up and sitting down, Boom Boom drove up in front of the house. He'd been trying to talk to her ever since that day in Personality but she had ignored him, brushing past him in the halls as if he were invisible. Now she closed her book and went out onto the front steps.

He bounded across the lawn, holding out a bunch of bedraggled lilacs. "Hey, how about a truce?" He was, for once, hatless.

"You know, you're just as bad as you were in fourth grade. Worse — you're old enough to know better now. I owe you a shoe in the stomach."

"I deserve it," he said, and held out the lilacs, a little boy trying to bribe his teacher. "Look, I brought you flowers. And they're not even stolen."

The daffodil he snatched off Armbruster's desk — when was that? How many aeons ago?

"Are you sure?"

"They're from my yard. Hey, look, don't be mad anymore, okay? It casts a pall over my existence." He rubbed his head, as if groping for his hat. His hair was silvery in the porch light, but there was something tense about his grin, something just a beat off.

"Admit you're a balloon-headed egotist."

"I am a balloon-headed egotist."

"And a bully."

"And a bully."

His big hand opened and closed about the lilac stems, and

Polly knew, as instinctively as she knew that he'd never admit it, that it had been very hard for him to come here. He was taking a risk; even Boom could be hurt.

"Well," she said, twirling a lock of her hair about her finger, "I might try putting you on probation."

His grin blazed; his shoulders unhunched. "All right, that's settled. Now come on for a ride. It's no night to stay in."

She stepped down, stood on the edge of the long rectangle of light the living-room window cast on the grass. Stalling. Trying to decide. She ran a finger over the bump in her nose. "Look at the stars. It's too bright here to really see them, but look, over there, you can just barely make out Cassiopeia in her chair. See?"

"We could drive out to the beach where it's darker."

"It's so warm! It must really be spring."

"The prom's only three weeks away."

"You know what I think of the prom, Boom Boom."

"I know you're secretly dying to go with me."

"Ho ho ho." She took the lilacs and bopped him on the head with them. The bruised flowers' scent filled the air around them. "You do, huh? You can read my mind, huh?" And I can read yours, too: Joking is the only way you know; pretending not to care is the net beneath your high-wire act, Mr. 3B. "You know my inmost thoughts, huh?"

"It's not too hard. We have a lot of things in common, you know." He held up his fingers and began to tick them off: "Dazzling good looks, piercing intelligence . . ."

"Sterling character, high ideals . . ."

"Lightning-fast wit . . ."

"Impeccable taste . . ." How easy it was to fall back into this, like falling back onto soft, fat pillows. "What else?"

"The sense to know this is no night to waste indoors."

"Wait and I'll tell Catherine I'm going out."

Mrs. Quinn nodded thoughtfully. From the living room Cass yelled, "Ask him if he's got any tie clasps!" and Polly tossed the bouquet of lilacs at her.

Chapter Twenty-eight

Within two hours they had been moving all her stuff back in.

From the dining-room window the Denning family watched them going back and forth to the VW, up and down the back stairs.

Mrs. Denning said, with a sideways glance at Naomi, who was pushing half a chicken sandwich around her plate, "I hope that's that."

Mr. Denning said, "Maybe we'll get our back rent now."

Gerald said, "Now that thumping will start again."

Stewart said, "How come Naomi looks green?"

Naomi said, "Why don't you all mind your own damn business for once?"

"Nice talk!"

But Mrs. Denning laid a hand on her husband's arm, hushing him. Naomi pushed away her supper and went to her room, planning to cry, and fell asleep at once, without even taking off her clothes.

"Thanks for taking care of him while I was gone." Tess had an apple blossom in her hair. When she leaned close to whisper in Naomi's ear, Naomi got a whiff of fresh-baked bread. Tess had never looked prettier.

Peter took the steps to the back porch two at a time, his arms full of groceries. Saturday morning, they had just come home from the co-op. Taken up their life right where they'd left off. To an outsider it looked as if nothing had happened.

"That's okay," said Naomi. "It was my pleasure."

Carrot tops tickled Peter's nose. Somehow he managed to shift all that food into one arm and put the other around Tess. There was no denying it: they were a couple. They looked made for each other. They beamed at Naomi as if waiting for her to take their picture.

The world goes two by two.

"You two look like an ad for vitamins," she said.

Peter laughed as if that were the nicest thing he'd ever heard. "Tess, did you invite Naomi up for dinner?"

"I was just about to. How about it? We're cooking up a real feast tonight." Tess slid her gaze up to Peter's face. "Sort of a celebration."

"That's okay. I have something to do," Naomi lied.

"I promise not to make artichoke spaghetti."

"That's all right, Tess — Naomi's gotten to love the stuff, haven't you?"

"Well, I don't know if love is the right word . . ."

"She tries all kinds of things she never would have before, huh, Naomi? Her tastes have really expanded. And listen to this — she's going to college!"

"That's wonderful!" exclaimed Tess.

Naomi moved toward her own door. Was that all their friendship had been? Just another of Peter's experiments? Hypothesis: Naomi Denning's mind can be improved. "I didn't really decide yet," she said, hand on the doorknob.

"We have to take her out to campus someday soon, so she can get a feel for what it's like."

"That sounds like a good idea." Tess shifted her bag of

groceries. "I think we should get this yogurt and stuff in the refrigerator, don't you, honey?"

"Uh-huh. Listen, Naomi, if you change your mind, come on up, okay? At least you can have a Twinkie — Tess lets me eat Twinkies now." He looked at Tess as if he'd said she could turn straw into gold.

"I'm glad," said Naomi.

"See you."

"See you."

Naomi watched them float up the stairs to their apartment. Last night was very warm, and they had left their windows open. Lying in bed, Naomi could hear music, laughter like tiny bells, and a creaking that was, definitely, not the swing thumping.

Someday, she told herself, going in, someday I am going to live in a place with no one above me.

Mrs. Denning looked up from rubbing the dining-room table with lemon wax. "Looks like she's back for good," she said gently.

"I guess."

"I bet they'll get married one of these days. Tess will want to, in spite of herself. Some things just —"

"Never change."

"I must be getting old, when my daughter can fill in my blanks."

"You're not old."

"I'm getting there." Mrs. Denning peered into the mirror above the table, plucked a gray hair. "Don't think I was eavesdropping, but — did I hear you mention college just now?"

"I've sort of been thinking about it."

Mrs. Denning grimaced, pulled another hair. "To study what?"

"Science?"

"Science!"

"I know it's hard to believe."

"Well, I do have a little trouble imagining you in a laboratory, when you can't even follow a cake recipe."

"I'm not interested in cake recipes."

"Ouch!" Mrs. Denning plucked one more hair.

"You should cut your hair, Ma. I saw a style in a magazine the other day I know'd look good on you."

"I should cut my hair. And my daughter is going to be a scientist."

"Whales used to walk."

Mrs. Denning turned. "I've been noticing a change in you lately, Naomi. You suddenly seem so grown-up. To think of my baby going off to college. No wonder I feel old."

"You could come with me. You could get a degree in business administration."

They both laughed. Mrs. Denning turned back to the mirror, pulling her hair up on top of her head. "Your father'd never speak to me again if I cut it. You start looking into college, and we'll see. It wouldn't be easy, but I know there are loans you can get, and, anyway, it's a year away. You might change your mind."

"Some things never change."

"All right, you. Here, Daddy forgot his lunch today." She picked a paper bag up off the hutch. "Why don't you surprise him and ride it over to him?"

In the driveway Naomi ran one finger lightly over the side of Peter's car. Peeking in, she saw the Dwight D. Eisenhower sugar packet still on the floor. The day Tess came back, Naomi's brain had been so foggy and slow, she'd looked at Tess standing there tapping on the window and thought, Tess must have forgotten something.

It seemed what she'd forgotten was that she couldn't live without Peter.

Naomi hopped on her bike and pedaled out into the street. Coasting down the gentle hill into Laughing Brooks, she rode no-handed. Saturday morning and everyone was out — painting, trimming, clipping, digging, removing storm windows like jewels from their settings, riding small children in wheelbarrows. Naomi took deep breaths of the soft, pollen-sweet air. She felt the sun on her back and thought, Life goes on, no matter what. Some days that fact seemed cruel, but today, just now, it soothed her.

Tess and Peter, right as rain together. Anyone, even Naomi's mother, could see they belonged to each other. Watching Tess come back was like watching someone buy a dress you'd admired for a long time, but knew would never fit you: someone else just the right size came along; the dress was made for her; how could you feel bad about her taking it?

You would have to feel bad about being yourself.

Naomi hit a bump, grabbed back onto the handlebars.

Besides, I never liked Peter that way. It was only Polly who put the idea in my head.

Another bump — her teeth clicked together. Well, maybe I did like him, a little, as more than a friend — it's true. But it's so obvious, now. He never thought of himself as anything but my big brother. All he wants is to show me things, give me things: the wonders of the water world, the idea of college, Twinkies.

After a while, Naomi thought, riding past Polly's house, after a while you get tired of someone giving you things when you can't give anything in return. After a while you don't want someone who's always running ahead saying, "Look at this! Look at that!" Always pulling you along behind.

After a while you long for someone who walks beside you.

She wheeled onto the highway, passed the mall where Wally's was. Polly should be there now. She and Naomi had barely said a word to each other since the picnic. They had stopped passing notes in the halls. Polly had begun having lunch with Boom Boom and his followers, who included Marcia Melon, and Naomi had taken to sitting outside by herself. She missed Polly; she felt bad for telling her to shut up. Every time she saw her with Boom Boom, Naomi thought, Polly needs a friend. But somehow — they both knew how — they kept missing each other.

Mr. Denning was so busy he barely had time to thank her for bringing his lunch. One of the pressers was out sick, Saturday was the busiest day, and the place was jammed with people waiting in line for the good suit, the dress for the party that night. Naomi stood watching for a moment, feeling a trickle of sweat run down from her armpit. Her father ran out from the pressing machine to listen to a man snarl that a button had been lost from his jacket. No wonder her father fell dead asleep on the floor every Sunday afternoon.

Outside the air was fresh and cool, and Naomi jumped on her bike and rode off as fast as she could. No. No! Suddenly she stood up and pedaled harder yet, caught by a glee so strong it amazed her, and made her laugh out loud. She was free, in the sunshine, and anything was possible. Yes, it was.

She careened off the highway and didn't pass Wally's, where Crow was trudging around the parking lot collecting shopping carts. He was wondering what was wrong with Polly, who'd called in sick that morning. As soon as he got his break, he'd call her.

Chapter Twenty-nine

Naomi sat outside the school cafeteria, eating an orange. She ate each section very slowly, chewing with great concentration. According to her new diet, this was an effective technique of appetite reduction. "Concentrate on your food," her new book said. "You may even want to count each bite. Deliberate chewing is guaranteed to curb your appetite."

Naomi moved her jaws up and down, up and down. From behind her came the dull roar of fifth-period lunch. Across the parking lot came Danny.

Naomi knew he had chemistry now, and that cutting Lee's class was suicide. The man had a sign in his room: ALL CUTTERS WILL BE PROSECUTED TO THE FULLEST EXTENT OF THE LAW.

"Hi."

"Hi, Naomi." He hesitated, standing there, obviously not sure she wanted him around.

"Want some orange?"

"Thanks." He flopped down on the grass beside her and took the piece she held out to him. This was already the longest conversation they had had in weeks. Naomi's calmness amazed her. She sat waiting to break out into hives, or profuse sweat. Instead, she went on quietly talking to him.

"You're crazy cutting Lee's class, you know."

"I know," he said glumly.

"Why are you, then?"

"I don't know." He shooed a fly off her foot and she saw the scar on the back of his left hand; she'd almost forgotten it.

"It's a nice day," she said when he went on sitting there,

staring at her sneaker (she never did get her sandals back) and saying nothing.

"I know."

She had to laugh. "I know, I don't know, I know — are you stoned or something?"

Then he laughed, too, and that was something she hadn't forgotten: that sound, like smooth sea stones bumping together. "I wish."

"Just spring fever, I guess."

"How — how are you?"

She shredded the orange skin. "All right. How are you?"

"I don't know."

From inside the cafeteria came the shriek of someone's laughter. Naomi wondered why he didn't go inside and see Marcia Melon. "Are you sure you're not stoned? You're acting funny. You're so quiet, you're making me nervous."

Danny sighed and pulled up a handful of grass. "These days I don't know what I'm doing half the time. I go around in circles."

Naomi didn't answer.

Looking at her foot, he said, "I cut Lee's class because Marsh asked me to. No, not asked — ordered. She said she's tired of watching everyone else eat lunch with their boyfriends, and she has to eat by herself. Do you believe it?"

"That's asking a lot of you."

"Ha, that's nothing. Every time we go someplace, Marsh expects me to pay for everything." Naomi reflected that Marsh was an even worse nickname than Nome. "And she's the one with the money — you know her father has the bucks. She doesn't like going out in my brother's car, either. She says, 'Look at the cars Boom Boom drives. How do you think I feel sitting in the back seat of this dump?' Well, that's okay.

She made one too many cracks about his car in front of him, and now Donny swears she's not setting foot in it again."

"Poor Donny. He's so proud of his car."

"Try to tell her that. Marsh has this problem: She can't get it through her head that anyone besides Marcia Melon matters."

"How is Donny?"

"He's okay. He gets on my nerves lately, though. Everything gets on my nerves. Sometimes I can't even get into working at the station."

"That's bad."

"I know."

"But you cut Lee to come here for her. You must really like her."

He moved his arms jerkily, spoke in a mechanical voice. "I am a robot. Marcia gives the orders and I obey." He dropped his arms. "You know what I think it is? She has to have somebody to go out with. She doesn't care who it is, as long as she's got somebody to be seen with. And wow, has she ever been in a bad mood since Boom started going out with Polly again."

Naomi gave a start. "What'd you say?"

"Didn't you know? I thought you and Polly were supposed to be best friends."

"Things change. You haven't talked to me in a long time."

"Yeah." He looked at her foot, which was just the same size as his. "A *real* long time."

Naomi put the pieces of orange peel into her lunch bag and carefully closed it up. "You better go in. The period is half over. Marsh will be wondering what happened to you."

"Yeah." He stood up. "Are you just sitting out here all by yourself?"

"It's nice here."

"Yeah, it is. Well, I'll see you."

"See you."

At the door of the cafeteria he hesitated, and turned to look back. She gave a little wave.

Chapter Thirty

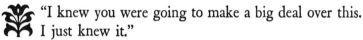 "I knew you were going to make a big deal over this. I just knew it."

Crow only looked at her, struck as dumb as one of the statues in the fountain. They were sitting on a bench by the pond, watching children throw bread and Cracker Jacks to the ducks and bloated goldfish. Polly and Crow didn't have any popcorn today; weeks ago Crow finally asked his father to stop bringing it home for him. They sat on the same bench they had a month before, but the park wasn't empty today. Today there were lovers everywhere, walking hand in hand, dabbling fingers in the fountain, reaching over the DO NOT PICK signs to pluck each other flowers. An old man selling balloons walked up and down by the gate, blowing on a little whistle. "Baaaaaaalloons!"

"Well, aren't you going to say anything?" demanded Polly. "I don't believe you."

She tried to laugh, but nothing like a laugh came out. "He asked me and I said yes, on the spur of the moment. That's all."

"But why?"

"I told you—because I felt like it. It's no great mystery."

"If I'd thought you wanted to go to the prom, I'd have gotten the money together."

"Don't be so dumb, Crow. If I went to the prom with you, I'd pay. We both know I could afford it better than you."

He brushed the hair from his eyes and went on looking at her. She turned her own eyes toward the pond. "I wonder where the swan is."

"I've never heard you do anything but mock the prom."

"I changed my mind. People do that, you know."

"I guess you must have changed your mind about a lot of things."

She turned toward him. "What's that supposed to mean?"

"Boom Boom's a jerk and you know it. If you're going out with him now, when you and I are . . ."

"What? Are what?"

"Don't pretend with me, Polly. Save that for Boom Boom." He stood up.

"I knew you were going to do this."

"Of course you knew it!" But he was yelling; she hadn't known he was going to do that. "You knew this'd kill me, how could you not know it? I've never pretended how I feel about you. All right—if you wanted to break up with me you could have told me straight. You didn't have to put your-self through the torture of going to the prom with that mus-cle-headed baked-brain—"

"You don't own me. Didn't I tell you that? I never ask people for permission to do what I want—"

"No, you just step right over them, don't you? Knock them down and step right over them. All that matters is what *you* want—you're so proud of that, aren't you?"

"I wish you'd stop shouting. You're scaring me."

"Nothing scares you. You're not scared of anything and you don't need anybody. You're so strong! Just like your mother." He stopped, looking horrified. "I'm sorry," he said quietly. "I didn't mean to say that."

There was the swan, gliding along the far edge of the pond. Polly saw it as if it were very far away, projected on a tiny screen. "Baaaaalloons!" called the little man. She had said yes to Boom Boom because, because . . . she couldn't remember now. It had been the demon. Now this argument was happening to her, she wasn't making it happen. She wanted to stop and say, "Let's start over," but she couldn't. She went spinning on, like a dry leaf caught on the spoke of a wheel.

"I never promised you were the only one," she said.

"No, you never promised me anything." He turned his back on her and she was suddenly afraid he would just walk away. "Fight me!" she wanted to say. "Don't let me do this to you!" But he didn't speak.

"You know what's wrong with you, Crow?" she cried. "You need *too* much. You don't know what it means to be independent and strong. You need me so much I can't breathe sometimes!"

He turned. "Maybe there's more than one way to be strong."

"You're always asking me for something, you're always wanting something, wanting me to . . . I don't even know! I don't know what you want, but you're asking the wrong person."

"No, Polly. If you'd give me a chance —"

He wasn't going to fight her — he was just going to keep on asking and asking.

"Go get yourself a teddy bear, that's what you need. And then leave me alone. I can't take it! I'm sick and tired of you thinking I need you, just because I'm the only one who's ever been stupid enough to go out with you!"

"I'm the one who was stupid."

They stared as if they'd never seen each other before. Then Polly turned and ran away.

Chapter Thirty-one

The next day Polly called in sick to work. "Again?" said Joe Atwater.

"It's Atwateritis — a terminal case," she said, and hung up. He'd probably fire her. What did she care.

Crow's break was at noon — when he calls, she thought, I'll hang right up. Noon came; noon went. He got off at six — when he calls, I'll listen to what he has to say. Six o'clock, seven o'clock, eight. He hates talking to me on the phone — when he comes over, I'll go out with him; I'll walk to the tree house with him.

Polly lay awake in her bed. Once she turned on the light and took the two photos — the one of her with her father, the one of her alone in the garden — out of her night-table drawer and looked at them. She fell asleep but kept waking up all night, dreaming strange, frightening dreams of avalanches and being buried alive.

When she woke early the next morning, there was a light dust of snow on the ground, and big wet flakes were still falling. Polly wandered around and around the house, looking out at the snow, and then at last she called him.

"I just wanted to know — our — the garden. Has the snow killed it all?"

"No. I heard there'd be a frost, so I went out last night and dampened the ground, then covered everything. It's all right. We — I didn't lose anything."

"Oh. I'm glad."

There was a moment when they both waited, and then they said goodbye.

Chapter Thirty-two

Naomi was very surprised to see Polly standing on her doorstep. She found herself blushing with pleasure and shyness.

"Come on in — we just got back from church. Want a doughnut? Want two doughnuts? Get them out of my sight — I'm on another diet and they're tempting me like anything."

Naomi was still in her good clothes, a pair of pale blue pants and a dark, crinkly shirt.

"You look like you already lost weight. You look really good."

Naomi's blush deepened. "Three pounds — through concentration. I'm really serious this time. Come in and say hi to my mother."

In the kitchen the windows were steamy and there was a good strong smell of coffee. Mrs. Denning stood by the sink, stuffing the chicken, Mr. Denning was buried in his paper, and Gerald was reading aloud from the comic strip "Believe It or Not."

" 'In nineteen twelve the Watchappee Circus Tall Man married the dwarf Tiny Tina. He was seven feet three inches tall, while she stood barely four feet high.' Oh wow, you wonder how they ever managed to —"

"Drink your milk," came from behind the Sports section.

"Well, Polly Quinn, what a nice surprise! We haven't seen you in a dog's age. Sit down, have some coffee, have a doughnut."

"Mrs. Denning, you got your hair cut! It looks great. Hello, Mr. Denning. Hello, Gerald. No, no coffee, thanks."

"Well well well. What do you make of this weather? Snow in May, what next? We've missed you, Polly — what have you been up to? I can guess. Naomi tells me you have a new boyfriend — what's his name? Robin?"

"Crow, Ma."

"Oh, that's right, Crow." Mrs. Denning smiled.

"Yeah. Well." Polly slid Naomi a look.

"Come into my room."

Naomi closed her door and leaned against it. "I'm glad you came, Pol," she said quickly. "I've missed you."

"I missed you, too, No— Naomi. I didn't even know how much till today, when I needed somebody to talk to so bad, and there was nobody."

Naomi sat on her bed. "What happened?"

"Crow — he's such an idiot. I can't believe him. I told him . . ."

"What?"

"Well, I'm going to the prom with Boom Boom you know, and —"

"No, I didn't know."

"Well, I am, just for a joke, you know — everyone will be there . . ." She stopped, remembering Naomi would not be there. "All of a sudden I just had this impulse and, anyway, Crow had a cardiac. He went crazy, right in the park. I never saw him get mad before."

"You must have known he would."

"That's what he said. Oh, damn!" Polly paced up and down the room, picked up a pillow and threw it down. "What's that noise, anyway? It's worse than Chinese water torture."

"That? Oh, that's Peter's swing. He must have just gotten up. He always sits in his swing and reads the Sunday paper."

Polly stopped pacing. "That picnic turned out to be really messed up, didn't it?"

"We may as well forget it, Polly. We weren't ourselves."

Was this calm, collected person the same one who'd been yelling, "I have a wart, I have a wart"? "How's Peter?"

"Okay. Great, really, since Tess came back." Naomi got up from the bed and took off her good pants. "At first, right after she came back, I didn't go up there. I was sure I'd just be the fifth wheel. But they kept inviting me and inviting me, especially Tess. She says Peter doesn't like to eat Twinkies alone." She hung up her pants and pulled her jeans off a hanger. "They're trying to work things out. I can tell they still have problems. Every now and then I can feel these little ripples go across the room between them, but I guess nobody's happy all the time." She sucked in her stomach, snapped her jeans, and looked up. "What are you staring at?"

"I don't know. You. You seem different."

Naomi laughed. "It's only three pounds."

"I don't mean that."

"You know what I think you should do? Call Crow and see what happens."

"Call him? Are you crazy?" Polly didn't say she had called him, and nothing had happened.

"I don't know what to tell you then."

Tell me I'm right. Two months ago you'd have said I was right. "Tell me if I should make long sleeves or none on my prom dress."

Naomi began brushing her hair. "You know more about that than I do."

"I was thinking we could walk over to the mall now and look at material. You could help me pick something out. It's pretty outside — the snow is almost all melted."

"I'm going out with Danny now."

"Really?"

"Don't get too excited — it's just for a bike ride." Polly watched the color creep up from Naomi's neck. "I asked him. I bet you never thought I'd have the nerve to do that. Neither did I."

"I told you you were different."

"Maybe you're right." Naomi spun around from the mirror, took Polly by the shoulders, and said all in a rush, "Polly, I think you should call up Boom Boom and tell him to forget it and then you should go over and have a long talk with Crow. There, I had to say that or I'd feel awful."

"I can't do that."

"Yes, you can. Boom could get someone else to go with him just like that." Naomi snapped her fingers.

Polly gently pulled away. "Hey, have a good time with Danny this afternoon."

Chapter Thirty-three

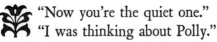 "Now you're the quiet one."

"I was thinking about Polly."

"Ms. Cool."

"It's more complicated than that, Danny."

"I know. I shouldn't say anything. You know her better than I do."

"She's hard for anyone to know."

"Look at those gulls. I always liked gulls."

"Me, too. The way they can soar, then settle down so peacefully and just bob with the waves. They've got the best of both worlds."

"I always wondered," Danny said, looking at the horizon, "how the Vikings and those guys got the nerve to sail out across the ocean. In those rickety little boats, not knowing where they were going—they must have been crazy! Or super-brave."

"I used to wonder that about the astronauts. Were those guys out of their minds, taking risks like that, or were they real heroes?"

"Crazy or brave. It's funny to think you can't tell one from the other."

"Maybe you need to be a little of both, to really be alive."

"It's good talking to you again, little sister."

Their bikes lay behind them in the sand. Except for some children throwing a stick to a dog, they were the only ones on the beach.

"It's hard to believe it was snowing this morning."

"Was that just this morning? It seems so much longer ago."

Danny wrote something in the sand with his finger, but erased it before Naomi could see. After a while they got up and walked along the beach, past the children, past the boarded-up concession stand. They had ridden their bikes for about an hour to get to this small, local beach that in a month would be packed with people. It was one of the beaches Peter complained was getting so polluted the wildlife wasn't worth looking at anymore, but to Naomi, it looked lovely today.

The tide was out; the wet dark sand was strewn with bits of rock and shell, like strings of colored beads come undone. Danny held his nose at the low-tide smell but Naomi liked that odor of worms and snails, jellyfish and crabs. Round holes in the sand marked the places where creatures had burrowed down to wait for the sea to come back to them.

They came upon a dead horseshoe crab.

"It looks like one of the dinosaur models I used to make when I was a kid," he said.

"They're ancient creatures — living fossils," she said, and bit her tongue. She'd promised herself: no lectures today, no trying to push her enthusiasms on him. But he surprised her.

"What's that — a living fossil?"

So she told him there were fossils of horseshoe crabs just like this one that dated back three hundred million years. "They're cousins to spiders — see the jointed legs?"

A little farther on they came to the end of the beach. They sat on the railroad ties that marked the boundary between the public and private sections.

"Remember that day we went to the woods? You were trying to show me things that day, too, but I didn't want to listen."

"Well, what's past is past."

"I guess I couldn't stand you knowing something I didn't. I liked being the one who told you things."

"I seem to bring that out in people." She buried her toes.

He touched her chin, turned her face toward him. "I acted like an ass."

She shook her head. "I'm glad you like cars so much, but I'll never be interested in them. You can't share everything."

"Yes, you can."

"No, I don't think so."

He rubbed his chin, and she knew what he was thinking.

"Even when two people have shared themselves . . . all the way . . . even then . . . I don't know. Maybe you can only touch someone else for a moment, only blend with him for a little while, and then your edges have to get hard again. Then you have to be yourself alone again."

She looked up, and saw relief on his face, the last thing she'd expected.

"I didn't mean to push you, Naomi. I don't know why I . . . to tell you the truth it was no fun for me, either, really."

"We have to go slow, Danny. If we go too fast, one of us will get gobbled up."

"I'm sorry I was such an ass in the woods, and those other times, I —"

But she didn't want to hear him say he was sorry. With a grin she gave him a push that almost toppled him into the water. "That's for laughing at me when I fell in the skunk cabbage!"

And she scrambled up and ran back down the beach, as far and as fast as she could, making the children's dog bark and the gulls wheel up and the wet sand turn white where she pounded her heels into it, hearing Danny behind her and then beside her, till at the very same moment they flung themselves down on the opposite boundary of this beach that suddenly didn't seem small at all.

Chapter Thirty-four

Maybe the strangest thing was how bad Polly felt about Naomi.

She was so unsympathetic! She couldn't have cared less. I went to her with my problem, and what did she say? "Call him." That was all. She didn't even try to see things from my point of view.

—She told you what she thought. What more do you want? She gave you her honest opinion.

I felt like I was talking to a stranger. I hardly know Nome anymore, and I used to know her inside out.

—Don't call her Nome.

See what I mean? She doesn't confide in me anymore. She never tells me her problems. And when I try to tell her mine . . .

—Didn't you hear what she said? "I missed you, Pol." You could tell she really meant it.

But she's been avoiding me.

—And *you* haven't been avoiding *her?*

I know I have, but that's only because—because I know she thinks I'm wrong! She's deserted me. And she was the one person I could always count on . . .

—Always count on to be your echo, you mean. But how many times have you told her, "You have to learn to stand on your own two feet, Nome. Stop putting yourself down, start saying no and taking what you want, not just what you're given." Didn't you tell her that time and time again?

Yes, but . . .

—She's only taking your advice, then. You did mean her to, didn't you?

Sure, but I meant with boys, and other people. Not with me!

—Too bad, Polly. Too bad.

Polly bought unbleached muslin and batiked it with a design of lavender and blue flowers. She bought a pattern for a long, peasant-style dress, and began to work on it. The prom was a week away. Boom Boom said they were going to the Bali Hai afterward, and then there was a big beach party at Pumpkin Notch. Everyone would be there.

Almost everyone.

Polly called in sick to work once again, and Joe Atwater told her she didn't work there anymore. In school she and Crow became experts at ignoring each other. In Personality he stared at the ceiling till Mr. Haight asked him if he had a stiff neck; Polly scribbled constantly. In the hall they looked away from each other, the way they used to turn away from his bedroom. Every morning Polly thought, Today. Today he will speak to me. The beans will be up, and he won't be able to resist telling me. Or he'll find a stone or a feather or the perfect strawberry, and he'll have to give it to me. Today, she thought, as soon as she opened her eyes each morning. She caught herself wearing the clothes she knew he liked best.

But nothing happened.

Polly took extra care with her prom dress, doing all the things Mrs. Armbruster had forced her to do in Home Ec, and that she'd hated then: she basted, pressed, finished every seam. Polly concentrated on her dress as if her life depended on its being perfect, and when she made the smallest, most undetectable mistake, she ripped it out and started over again.

While she sewed, words chased each other round and round her head, like the monkey and the weasel, round and round in rhyme with the up and down, up and down, *chicka-chicka-chicka* of the machine's needle. Fragments of their conversations ran through her head; the argument in the park replayed itself a hundred times, and each time there was one word that haunted her more than the others.

She saw Crow's face when he flung it at her, hair falling into eyes she had never seen angry before — her gentle man. "Strong!" he'd said. "You're so proud of how strong you are!"

The needle went up and down, up and down, all around the cobbler's bench. Strong, strong, strong. So strong come along King Kong, so strong so strong, sing a sad love song . . .

"Maybe there's more than one way to be strong," he'd said.

It was a word he used about his garden. Good, strong plants, he said, with good, deep roots — when you look at a plant you're only seeing the half of it. It's the roots burrowing deep and wide that give it its strength.

How was the garden doing? Was he working among the plants as compulsively as she was working on this dress?

"You know what's wrong with you?" she'd cried. "You need too much!"

But he hadn't called, or come. He hadn't even met her eye.

Then he said that about my mother.

Sitting at the machine, Polly tried to work herself up to hating him the way she had that day in the park. *What does he know about her, all the sacrifices she's made and the troubles she's seen us through? And all alone! Talk about only seeing the half of it. Sure she makes believe she's tough. That's courage, her way. She's not like you, Crow. She doesn't lay herself wide open the way you do, always trying to get me to tell you things the way you insist on telling me every* dumb thought that comes into your dumb head, always telling me you're lonely or you're happy or you're afraid of this or you wonder about that, always giving me things — gave me yourself, that's what you did — all your secrets and dreams, and now I can give you back the African violet and the photo and the shirt but I can't give you back yourself, I'm stuck with you — and even worse I can't get back the part of me you took — I hate you, Crow or Jonathon or whatever your name is — I hate your big nose and your messy hair and that stupid way your brows tilt up . . .

It didn't work. Her eyes grew hot with tears of pain, not anger. She grabbed up her dress and began to sew. Think of the prom. Think of everyone looking at you in this dress, think of dancing with Boom in his top hat. It was time to gather the dress's yoke. She had batiked it with a design of small, perfect leaves. Leaves. She remembered the fragile leaves of the tomato seedlings, the pleated leaves of the chard, the shiny new leaves on their beech tree. She threw the dress down on the bed; its artificial blue and lavender leaves suddenly looked ugly to her. He had ruined everything.

Something was happening. Polly had only sensed it since that day in Wally's when Crow helped her pack, but it had begun even before that. Something was chipping, chipping away inside her, something so small and quiet that at first she didn't notice; at first she took it for the beating of her own heart. Inside her a tiny chisel was chipping against white stone, and Polly sat on the prom dress she had taken such pains with, sat on it in her jeans with mud from the garden still clinging to them, and she began to cry. She cried because she was afraid she was going to fall into rough, raw pieces she would never be able to put back together again.

At last she fell asleep, and didn't wake up till Cass came

tapping on her head, telling her dinner was ready. Polly sat up and right away, before she had time to think, picked up the phone and called Boom Boom. She told him she wanted violets for her corsage, lavender and blue violets to match her dress.

At dinner Mrs. Quinn announced that the president of the Happy Lad Baking Company had written her a letter saying he was personally seeing to it that inspection procedures were tightened up in all his plants, and thanking her for bringing this serious and unfortunate occurrence to his attention.

Chapter Thirty-five

"I feel like we're going to a funeral," said Polly.

In the back seat of the Cadillac, Naomi and Danny laughed. They were laughing at anything and everything that night; Polly had never seen her friend happier. Naomi's prom dress was pale blue, trimmed with cream-colored lace, a whole size smaller than she usually wore. Danny's jacket was light blue; his carnation was white, and so were Naomi's roses. White shading to green — when she turned her head the velvet petals grazed her chin. Her first flowers. Huddled together in one corner of the wide back seat, they whispered and laughed together like kids at the grown-ups' party.

"This is like riding down the road in an ocean liner," Polly said, as the rustling in the back seat grew still. She peered across at Boom Boom. Was he glad, after all, that she had finally said yes? He wore his top hat and a tux with sequined lapels — a cross between a ringmaster and Mick Jagger — but he didn't seem quite comfortable. If you felt silly in an outfit like that you immediately began to look silly, and Boom Boom did, a little.

"What are you thinking?" she asked him.

He glanced at her, startled. "I don't know. It just came to me — after this there's only one more night, graduation. And that's it. Goodbye, Charles E. Sully. Hello, State University. Hey, that place is huge! They already sent me a student *number.*"

"You'll do all right. You always do."

"Famous last words."

She wondered if he'd bring his hat collection. She wondered what it'd be like to pull into a diner now, order coffee, and have an honest talk with him for the first time.

"And how about you?"

"Me?"

"What're you thinking?"

"There's not a thought in my head."

"You lie."

"I lie, I sit, I walk, I talk —"

"And here we are. This is your captain speaking, folks. Please fasten your seat belts. We are about to land at the Starduster."

In the parking lot Danny jumped out and held the car door for Naomi.

"It's only me!" she protested.

"What do you mean, only?"

The Starduster — Polly had rechristened it the Backbuster, because the prom was so expensive — was flooded with light. They went up the red-carpeted front steps, beneath the red canopy, into the lobby, where mirrors on every wall glinted with the reflections of crystal chandeliers and gilt wallpaper. Naomi shivered, clutching Danny's hand.

Everyone was there, and everyone was high, either on excitement, illegal substances, or both. When the four of them stepped into the Terrace Room, Tom DeMillo let out a cheer and toppled backward into the electric waterfall. Boom Boom's outfit created a sensation. Girls crowded around to look at Polly's dress. She had decided not to make sleeves after all, and for the last three days had lain out in her back yard, so that her bare arms had the first hint of a tan. She wore her hair long and straight, a few of the violets pinned in it and the rest fastened just where the yoke of her dress dipped low.

"You look beautiful," Naomi whispered to her. "You're the most beautiful one here."

And everyone was there.

Almost everyone.

Marcia Melon made her entrance in a strapless white dress, on the arm of a guy she made sure everyone knew was just home from college. She kept announcing this fact as if going to college were as rare as walking on water. She teetered around on spindle-heeled sandals, dangling earrings bumping her bare shoulders, breathing ice crystals whenever she got within ten feet of Naomi. Tom DeMillo exchanged his pants for a pair a waiter lent him — red, three sizes too big — and he ran from table to table, tripping over his cuffs and asking, "Is everything all right? Can I get you anything, ma'am?"

Polly did all the things people do at a prom. She danced with Boom Boom; she danced with Danny while Boom Boom danced with Naomi, who glowed, Cinderella. The band played "Part-time Lover" over and over. Polly spoke politely to the chaperons, even Mrs. Armbruster, who wore a rhinestone tiara and picked at Polly's armhole facing, and whose husband patted Polly's bottom as she walked away. She ate all the rubbery chicken and the little potatoes that looked like and had as much flavor as golf balls (the Starduster's policy was to pass off its cheapest food on "kids," who after all wouldn't know any better), and she gave her dessert to Boom Boom, even though she loved strawberries, because all the other girls at the table were giving their dates theirs. The only thing she didn't touch was the peas.

Halfway through the evening Boom Boom traded his top hat for a tinsel crown. He danced with the girl who was elected queen, a cheerleader with dimples, while cameras flashed and everyone clapped. Polly clapped, too. She clapped and clapped till she realized everyone else had already stopped.

"Come to the bathroom with me," Naomi said in her ear.

In the bathroom, which was called the Powder Room, they sat on red-cushioned stools before a gilt-rimmed mirror.

"I never thought we'd be here together tonight, Polly."

"Me either."

"My mother was so excited that I got to go to the prom after all. She must have taken a million pictures, I was blind for half an hour afterwards. She said, 'Oh, to be your age again. These are the best years of your life.'"

Polly plucked at her violets. "Isn't it funny how they only say that at times like this? Never when things are rotten?"

"I know." Naomi watched Polly touch the flowers, which were already half dead. Polly was having a terrible time. Anyone could see it. When she got home her mouth was going to ache and ache from all that fake smiling. But what could Naomi say? She'd told Polly not to come. You could give advice till you sounded like a broken record — the way Polly had lectured her again and again on independence — but no one ever really took advice. People had to find out things for themselves, that was all.

Polly looked up and saw Naomi watching her. She tucked her comb back into her small, beaded purse, Catherine's from long ago. "We better get back. We don't want to miss anything."

They didn't miss anything. They went to the Bali Hai, where Polly and Boom Boom sipped rum from a hollowed-out pineapple and had their picture taken sitting together in a big rattan chair. They went to Boom Boom's house, where Mrs. Bottzemeyer, one of her son's most loyal fans, fed a crowd a big breakfast. They changed into the jeans and T-shirts they had brought, Polly tossing away the long-dead violets. They rode in the caravan, the Caddy in the lead, that drove out to Pumpkin Notch. Boom Boom wore his crown, and Polly his top hat.

It was dawn. Slivers of gold were just beginning to show in the blue-gray sky. At the horizon a band of soft yellow light separated sky from water; it grew wider and wider; a shade was slowly being raised, a sleepy amber-colored eye was opening on the new day.

Naomi and Danny stood on the edge of the parking lot, looking down at the beach. People spilled out of cars, ran onto the sand. Some waded, crying out, into the icy water; a few tried to start a fire from driftwood and empty beer cartons; still others moved down the sand, hand in hand, to more private places. Naomi breathed in the sea smell, the wonderful iodine smell of the salt that now, as the sun touched them, glittered on the rocks.

"Are you having a good time, little sister?"

"You know I am."

"Sleepy?"

"Oh no."

He slipped his arms around her waist. "Want to go for a walk?"

His arms were warm and snug around her, and leaning back against him she thought, If only this moment could last forever. She felt his lips on her hair, smelled his strawberry-jam breath — for this moment there was no division. For this moment they were that third person, Naomi and Danny blended together. But if we go for a walk now — I may have to say no. Again. I may have to say, again, "Danny, I'm not ready, I'm not sure" — and maybe he will understand — he says he'll understand now — or maybe he'll be hurt. Then we will be two separate people again.

"What do you think?" he said in her ear. "Do you want to?"

She took a breath. She rubbed her wart. She turned in his arms — and saw Polly.

Arms folded across her chest, wearing Boom Boom's top hat, she sat on the guardrail at the edge of the parking lot. Boom Boom had already gone down onto the beach, and now he turned to call her.

"Polly! Come on!"

But Polly didn't move. Suddenly Naomi found herself by Polly's side.

"You okay?"

The top hat shaded Polly's eyes. "I told you proms were awful."

"It's not proms that are awful."

"This is how Humpty Dumpty felt, just before he fell."

Naomi gently nudged the hat back so that Polly blinked in the sun. "Know what I think? I think you already fell, a long time ago. Only you're too thickheaded to know it."

Polly blinked. "Come again?"

"You've proved you can make yourself miserable. Now what are you going to do about it?"

"That sounds familiar." A small smile curved Polly's lips, made its way up to her eyes. "You sound like me."

"Hey, the party's on the beach, you two." Boom Boom bounded back, retilted his hat over Polly's eyes. Danny followed him. "Did you see Tom? He tried to catch a Frisbee, and fell in the water — soaked to the skin twice in one night. . . . Hey." He stopped, looking at Polly. "Uh-oh," he said.

"Boom, know what?"

"I know," he said.

"I think I want to go home."

"I know."

"You do?"

"I told you I can read your mind."

"I'm sorry."

He drew a breath. "So am I."

Naomi turned away, sure Boom Boom wouldn't want her to see the look his face wore just then. The morning's eye was open wide now; it beamed the white sand gold.

When Boom Boom spoke again he was able to make a small joke. "But I guess a good man knows when he's beaten. Right?"

"You are a good man, Boom."

"So are you."

Polly took off the top hat. "It's not fair to ask you to drive me home. I'll hitch."

"Hitch! Are you crazy? Your mother would murder me!"

"I'll hitch with her," said Naomi quickly.

"You're not going anyplace without me," said Danny.

Boom Boom held his crown to his chest and addressed the sky. "Thus are the mighty fallen."

"It's okay, Boom, Nome. I can get home by myself." Polly started toward the road, but Boom Boom caught her hand.

"No you can't, Ms. Cool." He turned to Naomi and Danny. "You two can get a ride home with somebody else?"

"Sure."

"All right."

"I'll call you, Pol."

"Naomi." Later that day Polly would tell her, I wanted to say thank you, but I didn't want to start crying.

Later that day Polly would tell Naomi lots of things.

On the way home Polly and Boom Boom stopped at a diner and had a cup of coffee. At her front door, they kissed gently, and then they shook hands. Boom Boom doffed his crown. He floored the Caddy, and was gone.

Chapter Thirty-six

 As she walked to his house she thought of all the things he might say.

"Now that the prom's over you decided to come back? Well, forget it."

"What happened — did you have to kick Bottzemeyer in the stomach again?"

"Look, you hurt me enough already — please leave me alone."

"I thought you were too good to go out with me."

"What do you want, *icicle?*"

She turned down his street. It was still very early; she hadn't been to bed. The usually noisy street was still, with an air of waiting. A small dog quietly sniffed a tuna can; a round-eyed child in pajamas stared out from a window. She stopped at the lilac bush in front of his house. Most of the flowers were dead now, little clusters of brownish foam like the edges of waves at low tide, but the leaves were full and shaped like hearts. She stood looking at the bush, and then she went up to the door and rang the bell.

No one answered. She tried again, then remembered the bell didn't work. She knocked — once, twice, three times. At last she tried the knob. The door opened.

"Hello?" It came out a whisper. "Hello?" more loudly. Crow's felt hat, the crown dented in, lay on a chair. "Jonathon?" The word hung, weird and lonely, in the empty air. His father's black umbrella, the cracked spoke jutting out like a broken limb, leaned in one corner; the light on the ceiling glared down at her, daring her to snap it off, demanding to know what she wanted. *Intruder,* it said. *Too late,* it said.

A wave of panic swept over her.

"Crow? It's me!"

She was down the hall, past his empty room, into the kitchen, gripping the table and peering out the window — but the garden was empty. Empty and serene in the sunlight, the green and growing things oblivious to the thudding of her heart.

Something moved. Crouched down behind vines grown so tall she didn't see him at first . . .

The back door flinging open made him jump to his feet. She was ready to run to him, but the look on his face stopped her.

"I knocked and called, but I guess you didn't hear me?" Say you didn't hear me. Tell me it wasn't because you wanted me to go away.

He brushed the hair from his eyes, smudging his forehead — that faded checked shirt, his knees brown with earth. "I was going to call you today." His voice was so cold it cut her in two. "I have something of yours. Don't worry, it's not another one of my presents. It belongs to you."

"To me? I don't—" She took a step back, pretending to examine a tomato plant. "I can hardly recognize the garden."

"It's coming along." Without any help from you, his tone said. "Only there's been a rabbit. He's been chewing on everything. You wouldn't think a rabbit would hang out in this part of town, would you? But I've seen him. I've been thinking maybe I should stand out here and scare him away. You know, a real scarecrow."

The tomato flowers looked like yellow spiders; the leaves gave off an acrid smell. He twined a pea vine through the fence. At last, voice gruff, he asked, "So, how was it?"

"All right. If you were with someone you cared about."

He looked up, his brows making that motion.

"I never spent a worse night in my life," she said.

"Don't just say that."

"I wouldn't."

"It couldn't have been worse than mine."

"Crow, please can I hug you? Because my arms are aching to."

And then their arms were around each other, and Polly couldn't tell whether that choking laughing sobbing sound came from him or from her.

His glasses were steamy and crooked on his nose. "I've been thinking. You were right."

"Never mind."

"I was so afraid to lose you."

"All this time, if only you'd said one word—"

"You don't know how I wanted to. But then I'd think, You'll lose her for good. She has to decide for herself."

"Could you show me the garden?"

So much to say, but not yet. It was too soon for words. Arms entwined, they walked around the garden. A moment ago it had been a heartless place; now it was growing just because they were together, was shooting out those yellow stars of flowers, reaching up those dew-shined leaves just because Polly had come back. The peas were tall, taller than either of them. Crow paused, broke off a pod.

"I told you I had something of yours. Give me your hand." He split the pod, spilled emeralds into her palm. "Now see if they don't taste sweet as honey."

She laughed. She would never be able to resist teasing him. "I told you — I hate peas!"

"Quick now — the sugar turns to starch if you don't eat them quick."

Still laughing, she popped the shining green stones into her mouth. They tasted like honey — or as bad as peas had always tasted — or they had no taste at all. At the moment, Polly couldn't really tell.